Research **Prep.** GRE:

The Verbal Reasoning and Analytical Writing Measures

Research **Prep.** GRE

The Verbal Reasoning and Analytical Writing Measures

MCKAY RESEARCH

Kat McKay, J.D.

RESEARCH **PREP.** GRE
www.research-prep.com

Published by MCKAY PUBLISHING for RESEARCH PREP.

MCKAY PUBLISHING is located in Burlington Township, New Jersey 08016 USA.

MCKAY PUBLISHING is an independent publishing business associated with MCKAY RESEARCH, a textbook business located in Burlington Township, New Jersey 08016 USA. MCKAY PUBLISHING publishes educational books.

This book is for sale in nine countries upon its first edition publication.

© 2018 MCKAY PUBLISHING

TABLE OF CONTENTS

CHAPTER #1: The Verbal Reasoning Measure

- Sentence Equivalence Questions...13

CHAPTER #2: The Verbal Reasoning Measure

- Text-Completion Questions..89

CHAPTER #3: The Verbal Reasoning Measure

- Reading Comprehension Questions...167

CHAPTER #4: The Verbal Reasoning Measure

- Timed-Practice Question Sets..244

RESEARCH **PREP.** GRE
www.research-prep.com

CHAPTER #5: The Analytical Writing Measure (The Essay).....320

- "Analyze an Issue" Questions………………………………...…………326
- "Analyze an Argument" Questions……………………………………440

CHAPTER #6: The Analytical Writing Measure (The Essay)

- Timed-Practice Question Set………………………………………….529

CHAPTER #7: How the Test Works ……………………………………….546

CHAPTER #1

THE VERBAL REASONING MEASURE

Sentence Equivalence Questions

Sentence Equivalence Questions

Sentence equivalence questions require you to fill in the missing word in the sentence, two times for each sentence. You will use the entire sentence, plus the list of answer choices, to determine two answer choices that will complete the sentence and provide the same meaning in both completed sentence options. This is a context question: what does this sentence say as a whole? Which has a vocabulary answer: two vocabulary words fit the context and result in synonymous sentences. The two answer choices you choose do not have to be synonyms (the answer choice vocabulary words do not necessarily mean the same thing), but the completed sentences themselves must be synonymous (the sentences are alike in meaning once completed).

You have only one blank and need two answers. Each correct answer is a vocabulary word which, when placed into the blank, will give the sentence the same meaning as the other correct answer choice. Remember to choose two answers for each question and create a good quality sentence that means the same thing with both answer choices.

These are the GRE instructions that you will see on the test for sentence equivalence questions:

> **GRE Instructions: Select the <u>two</u> answer choices that, when used to complete the sentence, fit the meaning of the sentence as a whole <u>and</u> produce completed sentences that are alike in meaning.**

RESEARCH PREP. GRE

www.research-prep.com

Try one:

1. The book provides thorough and clear instruction without inventive ploys; it may appear innovative at first glance, but the book is strong because it is actually _____.

A	conventional
B	verbose
C	orthodox
D	vapid
E	untenable
F	exciting

Check the answer key:

A conventional and C orthodox are the correct answer choices.

The best way to get these two answer choices correct involves:

- understanding the context; and
- knowing the meaning of the answer choices.

The sentence context shows that the book is not innovative, and we are likely looking for an antonym (a word meaning the opposite of innovative). The context shows that the correct answer choices must be significantly different from innovative, and they must apply to a book.

The answer choices include the following words. Knowing these GRE vocabulary words will help you to fill in the blank (twice).

The Verbal Reasoning and Analytical Writing Measures

Answer Choice Vocabulary	Synonyms
Conventional	Typical, ordinary
Verbose	Wordy, overly communicative
Orthodox	Conservative, traditional
Vapid	Dull, boring
Untenable	Not defensible, unlikely
Exciting	Exhilarating, energizing

After working through each answer choice, we can see that the two that will complete the sentence synonymously (with the same meaning) are: conventional and orthodox.

Remember, you are looking for both revised versions to have as close to the same meaning as possible. You are also looking for each choice to fit the context of the rest of the sentence. Here, conventional and orthodox are both antonyms (opposites) of innovative, which fit the context. These two answer choices are therefore correct.

The correct answers will read:

- The book provides thorough and clear instruction without inventive ploys; it may appear innovative at first glance, but the book is strong because it is actually __conventional__.

- The book provides thorough and clear instruction without inventive ploys; it may appear innovative at first glance, but the book is strong because it is actually __orthodox__.

Try another one:

2. The problem was thankfully _____ by the hostess who interjected to end the argument.

A	exacerbated
B	ameliorated
C	exposed
D	overlooked
E	alleviated
F	animated

Check the answer key:

The correct answers are: [B] ameliorated; and [E] alleviated.

These are right because the context shows us that the hostess ended the argument.

The answer choice vocabulary words and their synonyms are:

Answer Choice Vocabulary	Synonyms
Exacerbate	Embitter, worsen, intensify
Ameliorate	Alleviate a problem, improve, make better
Expose	To show, open up, make clear
Overlook	Miss, blunder, lacking thought or consideration
Alleviate	Remedy, improve
Animated	Spirited, lively, with movement or excitement

Ameliorated and alleviated will both fit the sentence context and create two sentences with the same meanings.

The correct answers will read:

- The problem was thankfully __ameliorated__ by the hostess who interjected to end the argument.

- The problem was thankfully __alleviated__ by the hostess who interjected to end the argument.

RESEARCH **PREP.** GRE

www.research-prep.com

Research**Prep.**GRE

Sentence Equivalence Question Set #1

1. The view had always been breathtaking, but the new guardrail being installed threatened to _____ its aesthetics.

A	improve
B	compromise
C	support
D	espouse
E	ruin
F	falter

2. Despite the fact that the Earth is round, at one time this fact was widely _____, in favor of the belief that the Earth was flat.

A	recognized
B	argued
C	disputed
D	proclaimed
E	challenged

The Verbal Reasoning and Analytical Writing Measures

| F | marginalized |

3. While people can _____ birdsongs, they cannot successfully mimic them due to the significant differences between humans' and birds' abilities to vocalize.

A	explain
B	emulate
C	fabricate
D	imitate
E	relish
F	recognize

4. The _____ northern lights bathed the night sky in color.

A	glowing
B	stagnant
C	fleeting
D	unspiritual
E	evanescent
F	whimsical

5. The detective's search for evidence was thorough; still, she struggled with what seemed to be the _____ answers she received from witnesses.

- [A] evasive
- [B] tractable
- [C] baffling
- [D] unseemly
- [E] divergent
- [F] ambiguous

RESEARCH **PREP.** GRE

www.research-prep.com

Research**Prep**.GRE

Sentence Equivalence Question Set #1
Answers and Explanations

#1: The question was:

1. The view had always been breathtaking, but the new guardrail being installed threatened to _____ its aesthetics.

A	improve
B	compromise
C	support
D	espouse
E	ruin
F	falter

The correct answers are:

| B | compromise; and |
| E | ruin |

The Verbal Reasoning and Analytical Writing Measures

RESEARCH **PREP.** GRE
www.research-prep.com

The sentence context shows:

The new guardrail was going to diminish or worsen the beautiful view.

The answer choice vocabulary words and their synonyms are:

Answer Choice Vocabulary	Synonyms
Improve	Enhance, restore, make better
Compromise	Diminish, weaken; Reach mutual agreement
Support	Provide approval of
Espouse	Support verbally, communicate regarding
Ruin	Destroy, impair
Falter	Bring down, diminish; Hesitate

An additional note:

Notably, on this question, the word falter does not fit properly into the grammatical structure of the sentence.

#2: The question was:

2. Despite the fact that the Earth is round, at one time this fact was widely _____, in favor of the belief that the Earth was flat.

| A | recognized
| B | argued
| C | disputed

D	proclaimed
E	challenged
F	marginalized

The correct answers are:

| C | disputed; and |
| E | challenged |

The sentence context shows:

Even though the Earth is round, at one time people believed that it was flat.

The answer choice vocabulary words and their synonyms are:

Answer Choice Vocabulary	Synonyms
Recognize	Understand, believed known, identify
Argue	Dispute, disagree, to communicate against
Dispute	To argue against, to disagree with
Proclaim	Announce, broadcast
Challenge	A demand to explain or justify a claim
Marginalize	Downgrade, distain, disregard

RESEARCH PREP. GRE
www.research-prep.com

An additional note:

Notably, the word argued does not fit the sentence as well as challenged. The meanings of the final sentences containing disputed and challenged are also more similar then they would be if argued were to be allowed.

#3: The question was:

3. While people can _____ birdsongs, they cannot successfully mimic them due to the significant differences between humans' and birds' abilities to vocalize.

A	explain
B	emulate
C	fabricate
D	imitate
E	relish
F	recognize

The correct answers are:

| B | emulate; and |
| D | imitate |

RESEARCH PREP. GRE
www.research-prep.com

The sentence context shows:

People can seek to sing like birds, but their renditions of birdsongs are not successful.

The answer choice vocabulary words and their synonyms are:

Answer Choice Vocabulary	Synonyms
Explain	Clarify, explicate
Emulate	Imitate, mimic
Fabricate	Build, create; Tell a lie
Imitate	Impersonate, copy, emulate
Relish	Savor, enjoy
Recognize	Understand, believed known, identify

#4: The question was:

4. The _____ northern lights bathed the night sky in color.

- [A] glowing
- [B] stagnant
- [C] fleeting
- [D] unspiritual
- [E] evanescent
- [F] whimsical

The Verbal Reasoning and Analytical Writing Measures

RESEARCH **PREP.** GRE

www.research-prep.com

The correct answers are:

C	fleeting; and
E	evanescent

The sentence context shows:

The answer choices will describe a feature of the northern lights.

The answer choice vocabulary words and their synonyms are:

Answer Choice Vocabulary	Synonyms
Glowing	Providing radiant light, shining, beaming
Stagnant	Motionless, dull
Fleeting	Temporary, transient, momentary
Unspiritual	Part of this world
Evanescent	Vanishing, fleeting
Whimsical	Fanciful, funny, capricious

#5: The question was:

5. The detective's search for evidence was thorough; still, she struggled with what seemed to be the _____ answers she received from witnesses.

A	evasive
B	tractable
C	baffling

RESEARCH **PREP.** GRE
www.research-prep.com

D	unseemly
E	divergent
F	ambiguous

The correct answers are:

| A | evasive; and |
| F | ambiguous |

The sentence context shows:

Although the detective conducted a thorough search, she still struggled with the answers received from witnesses.

The answer choice vocabulary words and their synonyms are:

Answer Choice Vocabulary	Synonyms
Evasive	Elusive, to hide, to escape being found
Tractable	Docile, manageable, easygoing
Baffling	Confused, mind boggling
Unseemly	Unbecoming, seedy, without manners or grace
Divergent	Differentiated, deviating
Ambiguous	Indirect, vague

The Verbal Reasoning and Analytical Writing Measures

ResearchPrep.GRE
Sentence Equivalence Question Set #2

1. The provocative and stimulating play seemed sadly _____ when read by the monotone and dull narrator.

   A distorted
   B thespian
   C tranquil
   D insipid
   E terse
   F banal

2. The designer's creation of the chapel-length veil has proved surprisingly _____, as many brides still wear a veil of this length happily today.

   A frivolous
   B popular
   C serendipitous
   D formal
   E fortuitous
   F fortitudinous

3. The hero reproached his _____ twin brother when he found out about the twin's evil betrayal.

- [A] genteel
- [B] forlorn
- [C] perfidious
- [D] disloyal
- [E] flippant
- [F] cavalier

4. It is important to grind wheat into a _____ texture so that it can be used in recipes which require consistency.

- [A] homogeneous
- [B] natural
- [C] uncomplicated
- [D] heterogeneous
- [E] uniform
- [F] ingrained

5. Typographical errors in books occur rarely, but these _____ are, unfortunately, sometimes found after publication.

- [A] defects

B	mortifications
C	blights
D	peons
E	bohemians
F	derivatives

6. The amusement park had to close due to a _____ of customers.

A	grandeur
B	paucity
C	glut
D	flout
E	scarcity
F	din

7. Her reputation as a _____ book thief was undeserved; she was actually a kind-hearted librarian.

A	cordial
B	malicious
C	convivial
D	bourgeois
E	base

| F | malevolent

8. While he pretended not to care, his _____ was purposefully cultivated for the important meeting.

| A | demeanor
| B | exuberance
| C | nonchalance
| D | bravado
| E | indifference
| F | haughtiness

9. She felt plain and _____ as she stood near the bookshelf at the party.

| A | nondescript
| B | naïve
| C | ordinary
| D | nervous
| E | inhibited
| F | forthright

10. The movie producer seemed likely to be insightful and interesting, but when he spoke she realized how _____ he actually was.

- [A] venerable
- [B] obsolete
- [C] mundane
- [D] superficial
- [E] truculent
- [F] shallow

RESEARCH **PREP.** GRE

www.research-prep.com

Research**Prep**.GRE

Sentence Equivalence Question Set #2
Answers and Explanations

#1: The question was:

1. The provocative and stimulating play seemed sadly _____ when read by the monotone and dull narrator.

A	distorted
B	thespian
C	tranquil
D	insipid
E	terse
F	banal

The correct answers are:

| D | insipid; and |
| F | banal |

RESEARCH PREP. GRE

www.research-prep.com

The sentence context shows:

The exciting play seemed disappointing because it was read by a boring narrator.

The answer choice vocabulary words and their synonyms are:

Answer Choice Vocabulary	Synonyms
Distorted	Bent out-of-shape, exaggerated, untrue
Thespian	Theatrical, dramatic actor, pertaining to the theater
Tranquil	Peaceful, calm
Insipid	Boring, dull, lacking, unexciting
Terse	Short-spoken, abrupt, concise
Banal	Common, boring, unoriginal, trite

#2: The question was:

2. The designer's creation of the chapel-length veil has proved surprisingly _____ as many brides still wear a veil of this length happily today.

A	frivolous
B	popular
C	serendipitous
D	formal
E	fortuitous
F	fortitudinous

The correct answers are:

| C | serendipitous; and |
| E | fortuitous |

The sentence context shows:

The designer's creation of this particular veil has proven surprising in some ways because it has been worn for a long time; the original designer luckily thought to create it.

The answer choice vocabulary words and their synonyms are:

Answer Choice Vocabulary	Synonyms
Frivolous	Self-indulgent, silly, unimportant
Popular	Current widespread appreciation, having many friends
Serendipitous	Lucky, fortunate
Formal	Ceremonial, official, dressed up
Fortuitous	Accidental good fortune, lucky
Fortitude	Steadfast, brave, courageous

An additional note:

Notably, the answer choices add complication by using fortuitous (having good fortune) and fortitudinous (having fortitude) in quick succession. While the words look similar they are very different. Remember to look at each potential answer choice carefully and don't be fooled by similar spelling!

RESEARCH **PREP.** GRE
www.research-prep.com

#3: The question was:

3. The hero reproached his _____ twin brother when he found out about the twin's evil betrayal.

- [A] genteel
- [B] forlorn
- [C] perfidious
- [D] disloyal
- [E] flippant
- [F] cavalier

The correct answers are:

- [C] perfidious; and
- [D] disloyal

The sentence context shows:

The correct answer choice will further describe an evil twin brother.

The answer choice vocabulary words and their synonyms are:

Answer Choice Vocabulary	Synonyms
Genteel	Elegant, of high social rank, cultivated
Forlorn	Sad and alone, lost and lonely
Perfidious	Disloyal, to betray, treacherous

Disloyal	To betray, perfidious, treason (to a king or country)
Flippant	Without seriousness, fun and off hand
Cavalier	Without regard, arrogant, off hand

RESEARCH **PREP.** GRE
www.research-prep.com

#4: The question was:

4. It is important to grind wheat into a _____ texture so that it can be used in recipes which require consistency.

A	homogeneous
B	natural
C	uncomplicated
D	heterogeneous
E	uniform
F	ingrained

The correct answers are:

| A | homogeneous; and |
| E | uniform |

The sentence context shows:

The texture of the ground wheat must be consistent.

The answer choice vocabulary words and their synonyms are:

Answer Choice Vocabulary	Synonyms
Homogeneous	Uniform, the same, without variety
Natural	As it occurs in nature
Uncomplicated	Without complication, straight forward
Heterogeneous	Varied, dissimilar

RESEARCH **PREP.** GRE

www.research-prep.com

Uniform	Homogeneous, the same, without variety
Ingrained	Established, firmly believed

#5: The question was:

5. Typographical errors in books occur rarely, but these _____ are, unfortunately, sometimes found after publication.

A	defects
B	mortifications
C	blights
D	peons
E	bohemians
F	derivatives

The correct answers are:

| A | defects; and |
| C | blights |

The sentence context shows:

The answer choices will further describe typographical errors as a negative occurrence.

The answer choice vocabulary words and their synonyms are:

Answer Choice Vocabulary	Synonyms
Defect	Imperfection, deficiency, failing
Mortification	Shocking despair, humiliation
Blight	Destroyed, marred, diseased
Peon	Indentured or bonded servant
Bohemian	Eccentric, unconventional
Derivative	Derived from something else, unoriginal

#6: The question was:

6. The amusement park had to close due to a _____ of customers.

A	grandeur
B	paucity
C	glut
D	flout
E	scarcity
F	din

The correct answers are:

| B | paucity; and |
| E | scarcity |

The sentence context shows:

The amusement park closed because it did not have a sufficient number of customers.

The answer choice vocabulary words and their synonyms are:

Answer Choice Vocabulary	Synonyms
Grandeur	Majesty, to be grand or impressive
Paucity	Scarcity, lack
Glut	Large amounts, overfilled
Flout	To make fun of, mock, show contempt for
Scarcity	Dearth, shortage, lack, paucity
Din	Noise, clamor

#7: The question was:

7. Her reputation as a _____ book thief was undeserved; she was actually a kind-hearted librarian.

A cordial

B malicious

C convivial

D bourgeois

E base

F malevolent

RESEARCH **PREP.** GRE
www.research-prep.com

The correct answers are:

| B | malicious; and |
| F | malevolent |

The sentence context shows:

The answer choice should negatively describe the book thief because she has a bad reputation.

The answer choice vocabulary words and their synonyms are:

Answer Choice Vocabulary	Synonyms
Cordial	Gracious, with kind manners
Malicious	Spiteful, hateful
Convivial	Festive, jovial
Bourgeois	Of the middle class, conventional, materialistic
Base	Lowly, without manners
Malevolent	Evil, mean spirited

#8: The question was:

8. While he pretended not to care, his _____ was purposefully cultivated for the important meeting.

A	demeanor
B	exuberance
C	nonchalance

D	bravado
E	indifference
F	haughtiness

The correct answers are:

| C | nonchalance; and |
| E | indifference |

The sentence context shows:

The man attending the meeting cultivated a pretense of casualness (pretending not to care), while actually feeling that the meeting was important.

The answer choice vocabulary words and their synonyms are:

Answer Choice Vocabulary	Synonyms
Demeanor	Bearing, deportment, manner
Exuberance	Enthusiasm, joyful excitement
Nonchalance	Composure, indifference, cool under pressure
Bravado	Boastful and superior demeanor
Indifference	Uncaring, unconcerned
Haughtiness	Arrogance, boastfulness

RESEARCH PREP. GRE

www.research-prep.com

#9: The question was:

9. She felt plain and _____ as she stood near the bookshelf at the party.

A	nondescript
B	naïve
C	ordinary
D	nervous
E	inhibited
F	forthright

The correct answers are:

| A | nondescript; and |
| C | ordinary |

The sentence context shows:

The correct answer choices will be similar to, or able to coexist with, the woman's or girl's feeling that she is plain.

The answer choice vocabulary words and their synonyms are:

Answer Choice Vocabulary	Synonyms
Nondescript	Ordinary, plain
Naïve (naiveté)	Unsophisticated, untouched, sweetly simple

The Verbal Reasoning and Analytical Writing Measures

RESEARCH PREP. GRE
www.research-prep.com

Ordinary	Indistinctive, nondescript, alike
Nervous	Anxious, uneasy, tense
Inhibited	Reserved, internally restrained, nervously held back by oneself
Forthright	Direct, straightforward

An additional note:

Notably, nervous and inhibited make sentences that fit the context of the sentence, but not as well as the correct choices: nondescript and ordinary. The words nervous and inhibited also make sentences that are less synonymous than nondescript and ordinary. A person can be nervous while taking action, whereas an inhibited person holds herself back from action (at least to hesitate). So, nervous and inhibited are not the best answer choices. Nondescript and ordinary fit the sentence context more fully, and make two sentences that are more alike in meaning.

#10: The question was:

10. The movie producer seemed likely to be insightful and interesting, but when he spoke she realized how _____ he actually was.

A	venerable
B	obsolete
C	mundane
D	superficial
E	truculent

| F | shallow |

The correct answers are:

| D | superficial; and |
| F | shallow |

The sentence context shows that:

The answer choices will likely describe an aspect of the movie producer's character or personality.

The answer choice vocabulary words and their synonyms are:

Answer Choice Vocabulary	Synonyms
Venerate	Highly respect, worship
Obsolete	Out-of-date, outmoded, passé
Mundane	Usual, worldly, lacking an interesting or spiritual content
Superficial	Trivial, shallow
Truculent	Having a bad attitude, defiant
Shallow	Superficial, trivial

ResearchPrep.GRE
Sentence Equivalence Question Set #3

1. When she spoke with him, she attempted to appear _____ by feigning sweetness and unsophistication.

A	coquettish
B	immodest
C	flirtatious
D	tepid
E	crestfallen
F	lascivious

2. He respected her _____ way of thinking because it was unorthodox and not dogmatic.

A	doctrinaire
B	worldly
C	iconoclastic
D	tenacious
E	heterodox
F	subdued

3. One way to succeed on a team project is to _____ your team members' good ideas into a fully formed concept.

- [A] integrate
- [B] synthesize
- [C] herald
- [D] commensurate
- [E] synchronize
- [F] regenerate

4. When we _____ a political candidate, he has a better chance of winning the election.

- [A] complement
- [B] browbeat
- [C] assuage
- [D] rally around
- [E] guile
- [F] coalesce around

5. Her communication style was _____; he was bored and stopped listening.

- [A] grandiloquent
- [B] prolix

C	raucous
D	porous
E	loquacious
F	gregarious

6. The _____ in the speech were designed to add interest, but came across as mere chicanery.

A	rants
B	wisecracks
C	digressions
D	suppositions
E	pretentions
F	circumlocutions

7. His _____ sounded bitter and vindictive, but she maintained her self-control when answering.

A	vocalization
B	diatribe
C	temper
D	invective
E	prevarication
F	deliberation

8. The old _____ "make it or break it" seemed applicable when he "pulled out all the stops" for his audition.

- A maxim
- B tantamount
- C dictum
- D supplication
- E inference
- F didactic

9. His nonconforming approach to business helped him to become known as a(n) _____.

- A insurgent
- B mogul
- C businessman
- D devotee
- E maverick
- F inquisitor

10. As the _____ mountain climber struggled to reach the top of the steep cliff, her arms and legs burned from the effort of climbing.

- A neophyte
- B expert

- [C] athletic
- [D] chary
- [E] novice
- [F] decorous

RESEARCH **PREP.** GRE

www.research-prep.com

Research**Prep.**GRE

Sentence Equivalence Question Set #3
Answers and Explanations

#1: The question was:

1. When she spoke with him, she attempted to appear _____ by feigning sweetness and unsophistication.

A	coquettish
B	immodest
C	flirtatious
D	tepid
E	crestfallen
F	lascivious

The correct answers are:

| A | coquettish; and |
| C | flirtatious |

The sentence context shows:

|54|

The Verbal Reasoning and Analytical Writing Measures

The woman was pretending to be sweet and unsophisticated to come across to the man in a specific way. The answer choices show how she desired to appear and this appearance is created, at least in part, by acting sweet and unsophisticated.

The answer choice vocabulary words and their synonyms are:

Answer Choice Vocabulary	Synonyms
Coquettish	Coyness, flirtatious, sweet and modest
Immodest	Not modest, without modesty
Flirtatious	Coyness, sweetly and romantically attempting to attract another
Tepid	Lukewarm, nervous
Crestfallen	Sad, dejected, emotional letdown
Lascivious	Lewd, lustful, salacious

RESEARCH **PREP.** GRE

www.research-prep.com

#2: The question was:

2. He respected her _____ way of thinking because it was unorthodox and not dogmatic.

A	doctrinaire
B	worldly
C	iconoclastic
D	tenacious
E	heterodox
F	subdued

The correct answers are:

| C | iconoclastic; and |
| E | heterodox |

The sentence context shows:

The man respected the woman's way of thinking because it was different from others.

The answer choice vocabulary words and their synonyms are:

Answer Choice Vocabulary	Synonyms
Doctrinaire	Adherence to established doctrine
Worldly	Part of this world, unspiritual
Iconoclastic	Unique, iconic, individual

|56|

The Verbal Reasoning and Analytical Writing Measures

Tenacious	Persistent, relentless, gripping on
Heterodox	Unconventional, unique, unorthodox
Subdued	Not intense, calm, restful

An additional note:

Notably, in the sentence context unorthodox means unconventional and dogmatic means doctrinaire (according to established conventions). In the sentence, the woman was unorthodox and not dogmatic.

Additional Vocabulary	Synonyms
Unorthodox	Unconventional, not traditional
Dogmatic	Doctrinaire, according to established conventions

#3: The question was:

3. One way to succeed on a team project is to _____ your team members good ideas into a fully formed concept.

- A integrate
- B synthesize
- C herald
- D commensurate
- E synchronize
- F regenerate

RESEARCH PREP. GRE
www.research-prep.com

The correct answers are:

A	integrate; and
B	synthesize

The sentence context shows:

A team (or team member) is seeking to take varied good ideas and form a single complete concept to succeed on a group project.

The answer choice vocabulary words and their synonyms are:

Answer Choice Vocabulary	Synonyms
Integrate	To put together, take parts and make into a whole
Synthesize	To bring parts together to make a whole
Herald	Proclaim, announce, call out
Commensurate	Proportionate, corresponding in amount (commensurate pay)
Synchronize	Simultaneous timing, actions timed together
Regenerate	Rebirth, create again, re-grow

#4: The question was:

4. When we _____ a political candidate, he has a better chance of winning the election.

A	compliment
B	browbeat

The Verbal Reasoning and Analytical Writing Measures

C	assuage
D	rally around
E	guile
F	coalesce around

The correct answers are:

| D | rally around; and |
| F | coalesce around |

The sentence context shows:

A political candidate will have a better chance of winning the election if we do this.

The answer choice vocabulary words and their synonyms are:

Answer Choice Vocabulary	Synonyms
Compliment	Speak highly of; to make better (the wine complimented the meal)
Browbeat	Bully, crudely demand
Assuage	Soothe, ease
Rally around	Support, rally behind
Guile	Deceit, trickery
Coalesce around	Rally behind or around, create a coalition, combine with, support

RESEARCH PREP. GRE
www.research-prep.com

An additional note:

Notably, rally around and rally behind both mean the same thing on the GRE.

#5: The question was:

5. Her communication style was _____; he was bored and stopped listening.

A	grandiloquent
B	prolix
C	raucous
D	porous
E	loquacious
F	gregarious

The correct answers are:

| B | prolix; and |
| E | loquacious |

The sentence context shows:

A problem with the woman's communication style caused the man to become bored.

RESEARCH **PREP.** GRE
www.research-prep.com

The answer choice vocabulary words and their synonyms are:

Answer Choice Vocabulary	Synonyms
Grandiloquent	Grand sounding language; pompous speech
Prolix	Wordy, verbose, long-winded
Raucous	Boisterous, loud and disorderly
Porous	Having pores or openings, not water tight
Loquacious	Talkative, communicative, wordy
Gregarious	Socially energetic, over-the-top conduct

An additional note:

Notably, the correct answer choices prolix and loquacious create two sentences that are more similar than the second best possible answers grandiloquent and gregarious. Prolix and loquacious both mean verbose (wordy) *speech*, while gregarious more likely emphasizes energetic or excited *conduct* (such as gesturing while speaking). Grandiloquent brings grand or pompous speech into the answer choice set. However, it does not create a more synonymous sentence with any other choice than prolix or loquacious do together.

#6: The question was:

6. The _____ in the speech were designed to add interest, but came across as mere chicanery.

| A | rants |
| B | wisecracks |

C	digressions
D	suppositions
E	pretentions
F	circumlocutions

The correct answers are:

| C | digressions; and |
| F | circumlocutions |

The sentence context shows:

A speaker added something to the speech. The addition unfortunately failed to come across as interesting information or additional remarks. Instead, the portion added to the speech sounded like trickery.

The answer choice vocabulary words and their synonyms are:

Answer Choice Vocabulary	Synonyms
Rant	Rave, yell on and on
Wisecrack	Witty remark, joke made at another's expense
Digression	To talk off topic, wordiness unrelated to the point
Supposition	Surmise, suppose, guess
Pretention	Pompous, arrogant
Circumlocution	To communicatively circle around the point, wordiness, digression

An additional note:

Notably, the word chicanery (tricky, dishonest) in the question itself adds difficulty. However, it can be answered without knowing the word chicanery if you know the answer choice vocabulary. When answering difficult GRE questions, knowing as much vocabulary as possible is very helpful, even though there will still be lingering words about which you are uncertain.

Additional Vocabulary	Synonyms
Chicanery	Tricky, dishonest

#7: The question was:

7. His _____ sounded bitter and vindictive, but she maintained her self-control when answering.

A	vocalization
B	diatribe
C	temper
D	invective
E	prevarication
F	deliberation

The correct answers are:

| B | diatribe; and |
| D | invective |

RESEARCH **PREP.** GRE
www.research-prep.com

The sentence context shows:

He sounded bitter and vindictive when he spoke.

The answer choice vocabulary words and their synonyms are:

Answer Choice Vocabulary	Synonyms
Vocalization	Speech, oral sound, communication
Diatribe	Bitter criticism, a speech scolding or reprimanding
Temper	Fit of anger; To make steel weatherproof; To moderate emotions (to temper her anger means to reduce her anger)
Invective	Criticism to the point of verbal abuse
Prevarication	Lie, to tell a lie
Deliberation	Consider alternatives in an attempt to reach a conclusion

#8: The question was:

8. The old _____ "make it or break it" seemed applicable when he "pulled out all the stops" for his audition.

- [A] maxim
- [B] tantamount
- [C] dictum
- [D] supplication

The Verbal Reasoning and Analytical Writing Measures

| E | inference |
| F | didactic |

The correct answers are:

| A | maxim; and |
| C | dictum |

The sentence context shows:

"Make it or break it" and "pulled out all the stops" are examples of the two correct answer choices.

The answer choice vocabulary words and their synonyms are:

Answer Choice Vocabulary	Synonyms
Maxim	Saying, proverb, a well-known truthful statement
Tantamount	Equivalent, commensurate, the same as
Dictum	Saying, maxim, important statement
Supplication	Pray for, petition humbly
Inference	Deduce, conclude from evidence, read between the lines
Didactic	Teaching, educational, instructing

RESEARCH **PREP.** GRE
www.research-prep.com

#9: The question was:

9. His nonconforming approach to business helped him to become known as a _____.

- [A] insurgent
- [B] mogul
- [C] businessman
- [D] devotee
- [E] maverick
- [F] inquisitor

The correct answers are:

- [B] mogul; and
- [E] maverick

The sentence context shows:

He is known by the title shown in the correct answer choices, and this is because he has a unique approach to business dealings.

The answer choice vocabulary words and their synonyms are:

Answer Choice Vocabulary	Synonyms
Insurgent	Rebel, especially a rebel or person against a government or regime

Mogul	Powerful businessman (or woman), a unique or flexible approach with multiple successes
Businessman	Entrepreneur, business owner, executive
Devotee	Devoted follower, enthusiastically applying oneself
Maverick	A man (or woman) with unique and varied successes, nonconformist
Inquisitor	Questioner, especially a harsh or cruel questioner

#10: The question was:

10. As the _____ mountain climber struggled to reach the top of the steep cliff, her arms and legs burned from the effort of climbing.

A	neophyte
B	expert
C	athletic
D	chary
E	novice
F	decorous

The correct answers are:

A	neophyte; and
E	novice

The sentence context shows:

The mountain climber is struggling with the effort of climbing. Therefore, neophyte and novice are better answer choices than expert and athletic (which do not create sentences that are as close in meaning to one another).

The answer choice vocabulary words and their synonyms are:

Answer Choice Vocabulary	Synonyms
Neophyte	Beginner, novice
Expert	Skilled to nearly perfect at a task, better than others at it
Athletic	Good at sport or exercise, in shape
Chary	Thrifty, sparing or restrained spending or giving
Novice	Beginner, neophyte
Decorous	Dignified, regal, having good manners or bearing, acting with decorum

ResearchPrep.GRE
Sentence Equivalence Question Set #4

1. As an entrepreneur she excelled; she had a _____ mind for business.

- [A] biased
- [B] shrewd
- [C] prevalent
- [D] industrious
- [E] expansive
- [F] canny

2. A _____ glance at the newspaper was all he had time for today, since he was running behind schedule.

- [A] self-evident
- [B] effective
- [C] cursory
- [D] perfunctory
- [E] potential
- [F] visible

3. Vitamins can be _____ addition to a diet, as some help to ward off illness.

- A a misused
- B an efficacious
- C a significant
- D a popular
- E a useful
- F a minor

4. It is unfortunate that some companies treat whole grains as a _____, when they are simply complex carbohydrates.

- A quotient
- B panacea
- C cure-all
- D supplement
- E staple
- F vitamin

5. Her _____ was only outdone by her beauty, and that is why she won the pageant.

- A vocabulary
- B potential

- [C] intellect
- [D] confusion
- [E] popularity
- [F] likability

6. We must not _____ the effects of the disease by using medicines with significant side effects.

- [A] exacerbate
- [B] obsolete
- [C] increase
- [D] mitigate
- [E] change
- [F] comment on

7. The library book was on a high shelf that I could not reach: "how _____!"

- [A] ubiquitous
- [B] exasperating
- [C] incompatible
- [D] ruthless
- [E] frustrating
- [F] outmoded

8. Artifice was a way of life for the trickster who played card games for money, but his real character flaw showed when he _____ those whom he believed to be inferior to him.

A	extolled
B	lauded
C	belittled
D	intimidated
E	castigated
F	hailed

9. He admonished the clerk for providing the wrong document to the court; but at least his reprimand was _____.

A	judicious
B	brief
C	concise
D	pertinent
E	misplaced
F	reserved

10. The new painting was bright and fun but _____, rather than a timeless work of aesthetic genius.

| A | superficial |
| B | artistic |

| C | cultured
| D | mannered
| E | luminous
| F | commercial

RESEARCH **PREP.** GRE

www.research-prep.com

Research**Prep.**GRE

Sentence Equivalence Question Set #4
Answers and Explanations

#1: The question was:

1. As an entrepreneur she excelled; she had a _____ mind for business.

- [A] biased
- [B] shrewd
- [C] prevalent
- [D] industrious
- [E] expansive
- [F] canny

The correct answers are:

- [B] shrewd; and
- [F] canny

The sentence context shows:

RESEARCH **PREP.** GRE

www.research-prep.com

She excels as an entrepreneur, so she must have an acute mind for business, or an otherwise perceptive or excellent head for business.

The answer choice vocabulary words and their synonyms are:

Answer Choice Vocabulary	Synonyms
Biased	Partial, partisan
Shrewd	Canny, quick to understand
Prevalent	Widespread, common
Industrious	Hard-working, efficient, diligent
Expansive	Extensive, broad
Canny	Shrewd, quick to understand

An additional note:

"An acute mind" is used in the answer key. In this context, acute means keen or sharp.

Additional Vocabulary	Synonyms
Acute	Keen, sharp
Perceptive	Insightful, discerning

#2: The question was:

2. A _____ glance at the newspaper was all he had time for today, since he was running behind schedule.

A	self-evident
B	effective
C	cursory
D	perfunctory

The Verbal Reasoning and Analytical Writing Measures

RESEARCH **PREP.** GRE

www.research-prep.com

E	potential
F	visible

The correct answers are:

C	cursory; and
D	perfunctory

The sentence context shows:

The man could only take a quick look at the paper that morning because he was running late.

The answer choice vocabulary words and their synonyms are:

Answer Choice Vocabulary	Synonyms
Self-evident	Obvious, on its face
Effective	Producing the needed result
Cursory	Quick, partial
Perfunctory	Automatic, cursory
Potential	Possibility, aptitude
Visible	Can be seen

#3: The question was:

3. Vitamins can be _____ addition to a diet, as some help to ward off illness.

A	a misused
B	an efficacious

C	a significant
D	a popular
E	a useful
F	a minor

The correct answers are:

| B | an efficacious; and |
| E | a useful |

The sentence context shows:

Vitamins must be a helpful part of a diet because some vitamins successfully ward off illness.

The answer choice vocabulary words and their synonyms are:

Answer Choice Vocabulary	Synonyms
Misuse	Abuse, to apply wrongly
Efficacious	Having the sought-after result, helpful
Significant	Telling, meaningful
Popular	Well-known, favorite
Useful	Helpful, effective
Minor	Insignificant, small

#4: The question was:

4. It is unfortunate that some companies treat whole grains as a _____, when they are simply complex carbohydrates.

A	quotient
B	panacea
C	cure-all
D	supplement
E	staple
F	vitamin

The correct answers are:

| B | panacea; and |
| C | cure-all |

The sentence context shows:

That some companies treat whole grains as very helpful, while the speaker thinks that they are merely complex carbohydrates.

The answer choice vocabulary words and their synonyms are:

Answer Choice Vocabulary	Synonyms
Quotient	Outcome, remainder
Panacea	Cure for a disease, universal remedy
Cure-all	Universal remedy
Supplement	Additive
Staple	Necessary, basic
Vitamin	Nutrient, supplement

RESEARCH **PREP.** GRE
www.research-prep.com

#5: The question was:

5. Her _____ was only outdone by her beauty, and that is why she won the pageant.

A	vocabulary
B	potential
C	intellect
D	confusion
E	popularity
F	likability

The correct answers are:

| E | popularity; and |
| F | likability |

The sentence context shows:

She won the pageant because she was popular with the pageant judges, which is another way of saying that the judges found her likable.

The answer choice vocabulary words and their synonyms are:

Answer Choice Vocabulary	Synonyms
Vocabulary	Language of a person or people
Potential	Possibility, aptitude

The Verbal Reasoning and Analytical Writing Measures

Intellect	Capability of the mind, intelligence
Confusion	Disorientation
Popularity	Well-known, favored
Likability	Agreeable, easy to like

#6: The question was:

6. We must not _____ the effects of the disease by using medicines with significant side effects.

A	exacerbate
B	obsolete
C	increase
D	mitigate
E	change
F	comment on

The correct answers are:

| A | exacerbate; and |
| C | increase |

The sentence context shows:

The bad effects experienced by the sick patients should not be increased by using medicines with significant side effects. For example, a patient experiencing nausea from an illness should not take a medicine that also increases nausea as a side effect.

RESEARCH PREP. GRE

www.research-prep.com

The answer choice vocabulary words and their synonyms are:

Answer Choice Vocabulary	Synonyms
Exacerbate	Make worse, increase an effect
Obsolete	Out of date, no longer present, non-existent
Increase	Addition, growth
Mitigate	Reduce, diminish
Change	Substitution, replacement
Comment on	Talk, express, describe

#7: The question was:

7. The library book was on a high shelf that I could not reach: "how _____!"

A	ubiquitous
B	exasperating
C	incompatible
D	ruthless
E	frustrating
F	outmoded

The correct answers are:

| B | exasperating; and |
| E | frustrating |

The sentence context shows:

The library patron could not reach the book on a high shelf in the library, and she exclaimed regarding the experience. We can infer that she is not happy to be unable to reach the book.

The answer choice vocabulary words and their synonyms are:

Answer Choice Vocabulary	Synonyms
Ubiquitous	Omnipresent, seems to be everywhere
Exasperating	Frustrating, annoying
Incompatible	Cannot fit or work together, inharmonious
Ruthless	Cruel, mean without reservation, tenacious
Frustrating	Exasperating, annoying
Outmoded	Obsolete, out of date, old fashioned

RESEARCH **PREP.** GRE

www.research-prep.com

#8: The question was:

8. Artifice was a way of life for the trickster who played card games for money, but his real character flaw showed when he _____ those whom he believed to be inferior to him.

A	extolled
B	lauded
C	belittled
D	intimidated
E	castigated
F	hailed

The correct answers are:

| C | belittled; and |
| E | castigated |

The sentence context shows:

The trickster treated those whom he believed to be less than him unkindly in some way. We know this because his bad character is displayed most significantly by his treatment of those people.

The answer choice vocabulary words and their synonyms are:

Answer Choice Vocabulary	Synonyms
Extoll	Praise, applaud

|85|

The Verbal Reasoning and Analytical Writing Measures

RESEARCH **PREP.** GRE
www.research-prep.com

Laud	Praise, admire
Belittle	Disparage, put-down
Intimidate	Scare, frighten
Castigate	Criticize severely, punish
Hail	Honor, salute

An additional note:

The question itself adds the vocabulary word *artifice*, which means pretense, ruse, trick or deception.

Additional Vocabulary	Synonyms
Artifice	Pretense, ruse, trick, deception

#9: The question was:

9. He admonished the clerk for providing the wrong document to the court; but at least his reprimand was _____.

A	judicious
B	brief
C	concise
D	pertinent
E	misplaced
F	reserved

The correct answers are:

| B | brief; and |
| C | concise |

RESEARCH PREP. GRE
www.research-prep.com

The sentence context shows:

The only good thing about the reprimand was that it was short.

The answer choice vocabulary words and their synonyms are:

Answer Choice Vocabulary	Synonyms
Judicious	With good judgment, sound reasoning
Brief	Short, succinct
Concise	Short, to the point
Pertinent	Relevant, applicable, suitable
Misplaced	Displaced, lost
Reserved	Held-back, with self-control, polite but formal and removed

#10: The question was:

10. The new painting was bright and fun, but _____, rather than a timeless work of aesthetic genius.

- [A] superficial
- [B] artistic
- [C] cultured
- [D] mannered
- [E] luminous
- [F] commercial

The correct answers are:

A	superficial; and
F	commercial

The sentence context shows:

The painting did not have great depth or show true insight, but it was fun, bright, and new (recently painted or recently purchased).

The answer choice vocabulary words and their synonyms are:

Answer Choice Vocabulary	Synonyms
Superficial	Shallow, on the surface, trivial
Artistic	Aesthetic, beautiful
Cultured	Worldly, educated, advanced, knowledgeable
Mannered	Affected, artificial, inorganic
Luminous	Shining, radiating light
Commercial	For business or moneymaking, involving commerce or sale

CHAPTER #2

THE VERBAL REASONING MEASURE

Text Completion Questions

Text Completion Questions

Text completion questions require that you fill in one, two, or three blanks in a sentence or a short paragraph. Your answer choices consist of vocabulary words. Use one vocabulary word to fill in each blank. The vocabulary word answer choices are clearly listed; they show which blank you may fill with those word choices.

The best way to succeed on these questions is to develop a large vocabulary including common GRE vocabulary words. The GRE verbal measure is largely a vocabulary test. In addition to studying common GRE vocabulary words, follow the following strategy as you work through text completion questions:

1. Read the sentence or paragraph fully to get an idea of what is likely missing.

2. Consider your answer choices and fill in the blanks in any order.

3. Once completed, read the sentence or paragraph and check that it works as a whole. It should work as a logical, grammatically correct, coherent whole.

4. If it does not work, then check again for better options. Consider your answer choices again to change one or more vocabulary words.

The goal is to find the best vocabulary word for each blank and make the entire passage work as a coherent whole. Consider in relation to each blank whether a vocabulary word works in that blank, and whether that word choice goes well with the vocabulary answer choices for the other blanks.

RESEARCH **PREP.** GRE

www.research-prep.com

The study of GRE vocabulary words and their definitions is the key to success on this portion of the GRE. The English language has multiple definitions for many of its words. The GRE often uses word definitions that are more advanced than we are used to in ordinary speech.

Remember that each question has one, two, or three blanks. Each blank gets one answer choice from its own list, and the goal is to complete the passage to help it to make sense as a whole.

> **GRE Instructions:** For each blank select one entry from the corresponding column of choices. Fill all blanks in the way that best completes the text.

Try a text completion question with one blank:

1. The yoga instructor was an excellent yogi and teacher, but her _____ made her an unfortunately bad businesswoman because she regularly failed to arrive on time.

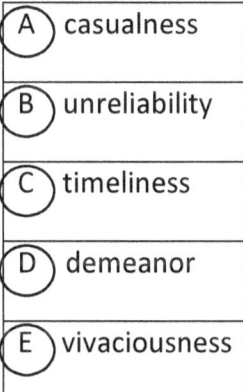

- A) casualness
- B) unreliability
- C) timeliness
- D) demeanor
- E) vivaciousness

Now, gauge your answer to this text completion question against this explanation:

The Verbal Reasoning and Analytical Writing Measures

The correct answer is:

(B) unreliability

Analyzing the sentence context shows:

The answer *unreliability* works in the context of the sentence because a person who is regularly late to teach classes is unreliable. It is also a better answer choice then choice A, casualness, because lateness is more closely linked to being unreliable than to being casual within the context of the sentence. Pay close attention to

RESEARCH PREP. GRE

www.research-prep.com

answer choice C, timeliness, and make sure not to confuse it with the word "timelessness." Knowing the answer choice vocabulary will help you to complete the text in text completion questions.

The answer choice vocabulary words and their synonyms are:

Answer Choice Vocabulary	Synonyms
Casualness	Relaxed, informal
Unreliability	Cannot be counted on
Timeliness	On time, punctual
Demeanor	Bearing, carriage, behavior
Vivaciousness	Social, exuberant, outgoing, an effervescent personality

Next, try a text completion question with two blanks:

2. The actor's (i)_____ monologue could barely be heard over the (ii)_____ playing and drumming of the band marching by.

Blank (i)	Blank (ii)
A) monotonous	D) clangorous
B) initiate	E) punctual
C) eroded	F) canonizing

The correct answers are:

Blank (i):

A) monotonous

Blank (ii):

(D) clangorous

The sentence context shows:

The marching band music drowned out the actor's monologue.

The answer choice vocabulary words and their synonyms are:

| Answer Choice Vocabulary | Synonyms |

RESEARCH PREP. GRE
www.research-prep.com

Monotonous	Boring, repetitive, unchanging
Initiate	Begin, start, create, originate
Eroded	Removed bit by bit, eaten away, degraded
Clangorous	Loud, noisy, resounding
Punctual	On time, timely
Canonizing	Consecrating

This second question was very vocabulary dependent; it can be answered easily if you know each vocabulary word.

Try a text completion question with three blanks:

3. Unfortunately, some science textbooks used in schools phrase (i)_____ claims as though they are (ii)_____ information, which can be (iii)_____ relied upon.

Blank (i)	Blank (ii)	Blank (iii)
Ⓐ incomplete	Ⓓ sensational	Ⓖ steadfastly
Ⓑ controversial	Ⓔ dubious	Ⓗ rarely
Ⓒ reliable	Ⓕ factual	Ⓘ avoidably

The correct answers are:

Blank (i):

Ⓑ controversial

Blank (ii):

Ⓕ factual

The Verbal Reasoning and Analytical Writing Measures

Blank (iii):

(G) steadfastly

The answer choice vocabulary words and their synonyms are:

Answer Choice Vocabulary	Synonyms
Incomplete	Partial, unfinished
Controversial	Unsettled, arguable
Reliable	Certain, can be counted on
Sensational	Exciting, causing a stir, amazing
Dubious	Questionable, doubtful, uncertain
Factual	Proven, reliable information
Steadfastly	Tenacious, unmoving, unchanging, strong
Rarely	Infrequent, unusual, uncommon
Avoidably	Unnecessarily, optionally

RESEARCH PREP. GRE

www.research-prep.com

ResearchPrep.GRE

Text Completion Question Set #1

Continue to practice completing the text with five questions:

1. When we consider what we (i)_____ to do in a given situation, what we (ii)_____ do is the (iii)_____ thing.

Blank (i)	Blank (ii)	Blank (iii)
A) predict	D) should	G) naïve
B) dictate	E) languish to	H) right
C) ought	F) use	I) assiduous

2. When time runs short, our efforts seem to be (i)_____ our need to (ii)_____; it is (iii)_____ to complete the task quickly.

Blank (i)	Blank (ii)	Blank (iii)
A) intensified by	D) run	G) imperative
B) exhausted by	E) care	H) questionable

|97|

The Verbal Reasoning and Analytical Writing Measures

| C) overwhelming | F) hurry | I) ambitious |

3. Our responses to violence presented pictorially in the news media can be emotionally stressful. Therefore, some groups seek to (i)_____ and even (ii)_____ the media's use of violent pictures on television and online.

Blank (i)	Blank (ii)
A) track	D) overestimate
B) erode	E) end
C) incorporate	F) rejuvenate

4. Instead of the (i)_____ conversation she expected, her companion poured out the sadly (ii)_____ details of his recent significant weight gain.

Blank (i)	Blank (ii)
A) controversial	D) apathetic
B) scintillating	E) invigorating
C) dubious	F) pathetic

The Verbal Reasoning and Analytical Writing Measures

5. While riding the regional train line daily, he had time to read classic books. Unfortunately, he found himself (i)_____ about past events instead.

- A) reconsidering
- B) considering
- C) procrastinating
- D) ruminating
- E) prevaricating

RESEARCH **PREP.** GRE

www.research-prep.com

> Research**Prep.**GRE
>
> Text Completion Question Set #1
>
> # Answers and Explanations

#1: The question was:

1. When we consider what we (i)_____ to do in a given situation, what we (ii)_____ do is the (iii)_____ thing.

Blank (i)	Blank (ii)	Blank (iii)
(A) predict	(D) should	(G) naïve
(B) dictate	(E) languish to	(H) right
(C) ought	(F) use	(I) assiduous

The correct answers are:

Blank (i):

(C) ought

Blank (ii):

(D) should

|100|

The Verbal Reasoning and Analytical Writing Measures

RESEARCH **PREP.** GRE
www.research-prep.com

Blank (iii):

(H) right

The sentence context shows:

The correct answers fill in large conceptual gaps. The answer choices help to iron out the meaning of the sentence, which we have an especially hard time understanding without the answer choices in this passage. Therefore, placing answer choices into the blanks in this passage is the best way to solve it quickly.

The answer choice vocabulary words and their synonyms are:

Answer Choice Vocabulary	Synonyms
Predict	To say what will happen, tell the future, explain a result ahead of time
Dictate	Order, authoritative demand requirement
Ought	Should
Should	Shall
Languish to	Lose strength, become sluggish, weaken
Use	Utilize, something having effect
Naïve	Unsophisticated, untouched, simple
Right	Correct, accurate, good
Assiduous	Diligent, dedicated but difficult

The Verbal Reasoning and Analytical Writing Measures

RESEARCH PREP. GRE

www.research-prep.com

#2: The question was:

2. When time runs short, our efforts seem to be (i)_____ our need to (ii)_____; it is (iii)_____ to complete the task quickly.

Blank (i)	Blank (ii)	Blank (iii)
(A) intensified by	(D) run	(G) imperative
(B) exhausted by	(E) care	(H) questionable
(C) overwhelming	(F) hurry	(I) ambitious

The correct answers are:

Blank (i):

(A) intensified by

Blank (ii):

(F) hurry

Blank (iii):

(G) imperative

The sentence context shows:

Time is running short and we must complete the task quickly. Therefore, the answer choices will need to support this reading and go together well within the sentence context.

The answer choice vocabulary words and their synonyms are:

|102|

The Verbal Reasoning and Analytical Writing Measures

Answer Choice Vocabulary	Synonyms
Intensified by	Make more forceful, strengthen
Exhausted by	Used up, drained
Overwhelming	Overpowering
Run	Move rapidly
Care	Carefulness, attention to detail
Hurry	Hasten, quickly approach
Imperative	Critical, important, necessary
Questionable	Uncertain, inaccurate, needing further inquiry
Ambitious	Oriented toward success, driven, goal-seeking

The Verbal Reasoning and Analytical Writing Measures

RESEARCH **PREP.** GRE
www.research-prep.com

#3: The question was:

3. Our responses to violence presented pictorially in the news media can be emotionally stressful. Therefore, some groups seek to (i)_____ and even (ii)_____ the media's use of violent pictures on television and online.

Blank (i)	Blank (ii)
A) track	D) overestimate
B) erode	E) end
C) incorporate	F) rejuvenate

The correct answers are:

Blank (i):

B) erode

Blank (ii):

E) end

The sentence context shows:

Blank (i) will have an answer that is a less significant response to the problem of violent pictures in the media then blank (ii)'s response. But still, both answers will be against violent pictures in the media.

The answer choice vocabulary words and their synonyms are:

Answer Choice Vocabulary	Synonyms
Track	Follow
Erode	Eat away, reduce overtime
Incorporate	Bring disparate parts together
Overestimate	Miscalculate, gauge by too many
End	Stop, conclude
Rejuvenate	Liven, energize, seem youthful again

#4: The question was:

4. Instead of the (i)_____ conversation she expected, her companion poured out the sadly (ii)_____ details of his recent significant weight gain.

Blank (i)	Blank (ii)
(A) controversial	(D) apathetic
(B) scintillating	(E) invigorating
(C) dubious	(F) pathetic

The correct answers are:

Blank (i):

(B) scintillating

Blank (ii):

(F) pathetic

RESEARCH **PREP.** GRE

www.research-prep.com

The sentence context shows:

The sad details discussed by the man were a negative contrast to the positive conversation the woman expected to have.

The answer choice vocabulary words and their synonyms are:

Answer Choice Vocabulary	Synonyms
Controversial	Unsettled, arguable
Scintillating	Engaging, sparkling
Dubious	Questionable, doubtful
Apathetic	Indifferent, uncaring, disengaged
Invigorating	Energizing, exciting
Pathetic	Pitiable, sad, causing compassion

#5: The question was:

5. While riding the regional train line daily, he had time to read classic books. Unfortunately, he found himself (i)_____ about past events instead.

- A) reconsidering
- B) considering
- C) procrastinating
- D) ruminating
- E) prevaricating

The Verbal Reasoning and Analytical Writing Measures

The correct answer is:

Ⓓ ruminating

The sentence context shows:

The man did not read because he fell into negative thoughts about past events.

The answer choice vocabulary words and their synonyms are:

Answer Choice Vocabulary	Synonyms
Reconsidering	Mull over, ponder repeatedly
Considering	Ponder, think about
Procrastinating	To delay, postpone
Ruminating	Think about seriously, brood
Prevaricating	Lying

Now that you have had some practice, remember that the sentence context for all text completion questions involves this key:

The key to text completion questions is to make sure that you know the vocabulary. Continue to learn GRE answer choice vocabulary words to get better at completing the text. Then, make sure that the words you choose will fill in the blanks in a way that creates a consistent sentence or paragraph.

- Know the vocabulary words; and
- Make sure that the vocabulary words you choose all work together.

ResearchPrep.GRE

Text Completion Question Set #2

1. The fashion designer sought to create classic, timeless dresses, but unfortunately they seemed _____ to many prospective customers.

- A) iconoclastic
- B) commonplace
- C) luminous
- D) inconsistent
- E) splendid

2. His professor said that the text is deep and interesting, (i)_____ difficult to read. However the student was confused by the (ii)_____ text.

Blank (i)	Blank (ii)
A) invitingly	D) straightforward
B) albeit	E) trivial
C) scintillatingly	F) abstruse

3. The library's efforts to (i)_____ the sounds of students' cell phones seemed like it should be (ii)_____. However, it was proving difficult because of (iii)_____ students who refused to cooperate.

Blank (i)	Blank (ii)	Blank (iii)
A) quell	D) spartan	G) slovenly
B) abase	E) easy	H) recalcitrant
C) exhaust	F) cacophonous	I) spurious

4. Her _____ of the modern artist was irksome to her boyfriend, the plain staid chemist who wanted his girlfriend all to himself.

A) castigation
B) idyllic
C) portrayal
D) idolatry
E) nadir

5. It was very difficult for the new professor to overcome her (i)_____ despite her attempts to be overt and (ii)_____.

Blank (i)	Blank (ii)
A) diffidence	D) officious
B) obliviousness	E) paltry
C) fluency	F) forthright

6. The research company's policy was to hire the most careful researchers. However, it was difficult to gauge (i)_____ attention to (ii)_____ from applicants' (iii)_____ about themselves. So, they obtained examples of applicants' work.

Blank (i)	Blank (ii)	Blank (iii)
A) quiet	D) detail	G) recriminations
B) tyrannical	E) truisms	H) communications
C) painstaking	F) windfalls	I) refutations

7. Biodiversity in well-forested areas is (i)_____ to fully assess because of the (ii)_____ of (iii)_____ plants and animals in forests.

|111|

Blank (i)	Blank (ii)	Blank (iii)
A) tumultuous	D) vexing	G) conversant
B) daunting	E) decorum	H) indigenous
C) simple	F) multitude	I) indigent

8. Communication systems created by Plexus McKay were some of the most specialized and sophisticated systems of their _____.

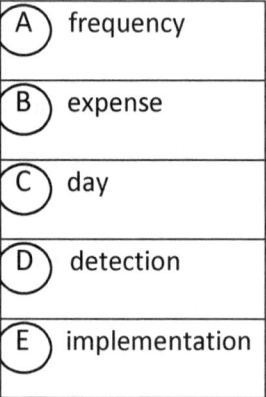

A) frequency
B) expense
C) day
D) detection
E) implementation

9. The collected works of the philosopher Plato are voluminous, but because Plato's philosophy is so interesting and (i)_____ to read, students find themselves learning a great deal from the (ii)_____ texts without feeling like they are studying.

	Blank (i)		Blank (ii)
A	veracious	D	erudite
B	engaging	E	impenetrable
C	incendiary	F	questionable

10. The caterpillar's (i)_____ into a butterfly is a (ii)_____, careful biological change of each part of the (iii)_____ into its new form.

	Blank (i)		Blank (ii)		Blank (iii)
A	revision	D	meticulous	G	sophist
B	vacillation	E	slothful	H	organism
C	metamorphosis	F	fickle	I	hedonist

RESEARCH **PREP.** GRE

www.research-prep.com

Research**Prep.**GRE

Text Completion Question Set #2

Answers and Explanations

#1: The question was:

1. The fashion designer sought to create classic, timeless dresses, but unfortunately they seemed _____ to many prospective customers.

- (A) iconoclastic
- (B) commonplace
- (C) luminous
- (D) inconsistent
- (E) splendid

The correct answer is:

(B) commonplace

|114|

The Verbal Reasoning and Analytical Writing Measures

RESEARCH PREP. GRE

www.research-prep.com

The answer choice vocabulary words and their synonyms are:

Answer Choice Vocabulary	Synonyms
Iconoclastic	Unique, setting a new standard, different from tradition
Commonplace	Boring, regular
Luminous	Glowing, shining light
Inconsistent	Sporadic, divergent, not uniform, self-contradicting
Splendid	Beautiful, excellent, wonderful

#2: The question was:

2. His professor said that the text is deep and interesting, (i)_____ difficult to read. However the student was confused by the (ii)_____ text.

Blank (i)	Blank (ii)
A) invitingly	D) straightforward
B) albeit	E) trivial
C) scintillatingly	F) abstruse

The correct answers are:

Blank (i):

B) albeit

Blank (ii):

F) abstruse

The Verbal Reasoning and Analytical Writing Measures

The answer choice vocabulary words and their synonyms are:

Answer Choice Vocabulary	Synonyms
Invitingly	Engaging, friendly
Albeit	But, while still being, while also
Scintillatingly	Engaging, sparkling
Straightforward	Simple, easy
Trivial	Unimportant, trifling
Abstruse	Profound, difficult

#3: The question was:

A) quell	D) spartan	G) slovenly
B) abase	E) easy	H) recalcitrant
C) exhaust	F) cacophonous	I) spurious

The correct answers are:

Blank (i):

A) quell

Blank (ii):

E) easy

Blank (iii):

H) recalcitrant

RESEARCH PREP. GRE
www.research-prep.com

The answer choice vocabulary words and their synonyms are:

Answer Choice Vocabulary	Synonyms
Quell	Quiet, moderate, put down
Abase	Humiliate, lessen
Exhaust	Tire out, use up
Spartan	Bare, without luxury
Easy	Simple, straightforward
Cacophonous	Discordant
Slovenly	Messy due to laziness, unkempt
Recalcitrant	Obstinate, stubborn, resistant
Spurious	False, counterfeit

#4: The question was:

4. Her _____ of the modern artist was irksome to her boyfriend, the plain staid chemist who wanted his girlfriend all to himself.

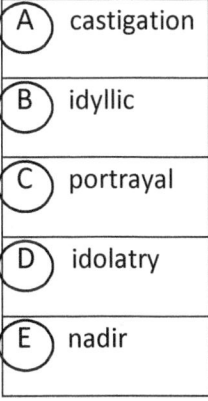

A) castigation
B) idyllic
C) portrayal
D) idolatry
E) nadir

The correct answer is:

D) idolatry

The Verbal Reasoning and Analytical Writing Measures

The answer choice vocabulary words and their synonyms are:

Answer Choice Vocabulary	Synonyms
Castigation	Severe criticism, berating, yelling and scolding
Idyllic	Without flaw, beautiful and carefree
Portrayal	Depiction
Idolatry	Non-religious worship, boundless admiration, love of things
Nadir	Rock bottom, a low point

RESEARCH PREP. GRE
www.research-prep.com

#5: The question was:

5. It was very difficult for the new professor to overcome her (i)_____ despite her attempts to be overt and (ii)_____.

Blank (i)	Blank (ii)
(A) diffidence	(D) officious
(B) obliviousness	(E) paltry
(C) fluency	(F) forthright

The correct answers are:

Blank (i):

(A) diffidence

Blank (ii):

(F) forthright

The answer choice vocabulary words and their synonyms are:

Answer Choice Vocabulary	Synonyms
Diffidence	Shyness
Obliviousness	Mental absorption elsewhere, unaware of current surroundings
Fluency	Flowing speech, excellent knowledge of a language

The Verbal Reasoning and Analytical Writing Measures

Officious	Pushy, overly engaged, meddlesome
Paltry	Trifling, insignificant
Forthright	Direct, straightforward

#6: The question was:

6. The research company's policy was to hire the most careful researchers. However, it was difficult to gauge (i)_____ attention to (ii)_____ from applicants' (iii)_____ about themselves. So, they obtained examples of applicants' work.

	Blank (i)		Blank (ii)		Blank (iii)
A	quiet	D	detail	G	recriminations
B	tyrannical	E	truisms	H	communications
C	painstaking	F	windfalls	I	refutations

The correct answers are:

Blank (i):

C) painstaking

Blank (ii):

D) detail

Blank (iii):

H) communications

RESEARCH PREP. GRE
www.research-prep.com

The answer choice vocabulary words and their synonyms are:

Answer Choice Vocabulary	Synonyms
Quiet	Without or very little sound, silence
Tyrannical	Oppressive, cruel, ruling automatically
Painstaking	Careful attention, devotion to one's work
Detail	Feature, specific aspect
Truisms	Pithy truthful statements
Windfalls	Lucky winnings, underserved benefits
Recriminations	Countercharges, argument against accusations
Communications	Systems of exchanging information
Refutations	Statements to disprove (to refute)

#7: The question was:

7. Biodiversity in well-forested areas is (i)_____ to fully assess because of the (ii)_____ of (iii)_____ plants and animals in forests.

Blank (i)	Blank (ii)	Blank (iii)
A) tumultuous	D) vexing	G) conversant
B) daunting	E) decorum	H) indigenous
C) simple	F) multitude	I) indigent

The Verbal Reasoning and Analytical Writing Measures

The correct answers are:

Blank (i):

(B) daunting

Blank (ii):

(F) multitude

Blank (iii):

(H) indigenous

The answer choice vocabulary words and their synonyms are:

Answer Choice Vocabulary	Synonyms
Tumultuous	Commotion, an uproar, riotous
Daunting	Intimidating, nerve-wracking
Simple	Easy, straightforward
Vexing	Stressing, causing distress
Decorum	Having manners, acting properly
Multitude	Numerous, multiplicity, many
Conversant	Familiarity, understanding
Indigenous	Native, originating in the place
Indigent	Poor, without money

#8: The question was:

8. Communication systems created by Plexus McKay were some of the most specialized and sophisticated systems of their _____.

RESEARCH PREP. GRE

www.research-prep.com

A	frequency
B	expense
C	day
D	detection
E	implementation

The correct answer is:

 day

The answer choice vocabulary words and their synonyms are:

Answer Choice Vocabulary	Synonyms
Frequency	Commonness, repetitiveness
Expense	Cost, payment
Day	Timeframe, light part of every 24 hours
Detection	Discovery, to find
Implementation	Put something into effect, begin

#9: The question was:

9. The collected works of the philosopher Plato are voluminous, but because Plato's philosophy is so interesting and (i)_____ to read, students find themselves learning a great deal from the (ii)_____ texts without feeling like they are studying.

	Blank (i)		Blank (ii)
(A)	veracious	(D)	erudite
(B)	engaging	(E)	impenetrable
(C)	incendiary	(F)	questionable

The correct answers are:

Blank (i):

(B) engaging

Blank (ii):

(D) erudite

The answer choice vocabulary words and their synonyms are:

Answer Choice Vocabulary	Synonyms
Veracious	Honest, truthful
Engaging	Involving, attracting, contacting
Incendiary	Flammable, volatile
Erudite	Scholarly
Impenetrable	Cannot be entered, cannot be understood
Questionable	Uncertain, not fully determined

#10: The question was:

RESEARCH PREP. GRE
www.research-prep.com

10. The caterpillar's (i)_____ into a butterfly is a (ii)_____, careful biological change of each part of the (iii)_____ into its new form.

Blank (i)	Blank (ii)	Blank (iii)
A) revision	D) meticulous	G) sophist
B) vacillation	E) slothful	H) organism
C) metamorphosis	F) fickle	I) hedonist

The correct answers are:

Blank (i):

C) metamorphosis

Blank (ii):

D) meticulous

Blank (iii):

H) organism

The answer choice vocabulary words and their synonyms are:

Answer Choice Vocabulary	Synonyms
Revision	Change, modification
Vacillation	Fluctuate, change repeatedly
Metamorphosis	Changing through stages & development
Meticulous	Careful, attention to detail, painstaking
Slothful	Lazy

The Verbal Reasoning and Analytical Writing Measures

Fickle	Uncertain, unsatisfied, repeatedly changing one's mind
Sophist	Ancient tutor or teacher, presenter of an argument
Organism	Plant or animal (even unicellular)
Hedonist	Pleasure-oriented person

ResearchPrep.GRE

Text Completion Question Set #3

1. After describing the author as anything other than insignificant, the book review changed when describing the movie made about her work, which was_____.

- A) significant
- B) dynamic
- C) brilliant
- D) ingenious
- E) feckless

2. The bank created pamphlets explaining (i)_____ and (ii)_____ to help families create budgets and stick to them in the economic downturn.

Blank (i)	Blank (ii)
A) proxy	D) economy
B) wealth	E) frustration
C) frugality	F) fortitude

3. The movie industry transitioned from silent films to "talkies" so long ago that many children (i)_____ do not (ii)_____ the (iii)_____ silent films.

Blank (i)	Blank (ii)	Blank (iii)
A) omnisciently	D) recall	G) provincial
B) contemporaneously	E) rapport	H) outmoded
C) today	F) query	I) outspoken

4. During the world wars _____ were sometimes imprisoned for their refusal to become soldiers, but they would also serve in non-arms bearing capacities such as, serving as medical personnel.

A) sages
B) hypochondriacs
C) pacifists
D) plebeians
E) philanthropists

RESEARCH PREP. GRE
www.research-prep.com

5. Walden pond was calm and placid, a place where Henry David Thoreau could likewise remain (i)_____ by leaving behind the insolent and (ii)_____ people who cause disruption in everyday life.

Blank (i)	Blank (ii)
A) dauntless	D) impertinent
B) poignant	E) helpful
C) imperturbable	F) reverent

6. Van Gogh's work displayed his (i)_____ artistic skill and heartfelt (ii)_____ which is why his paintings of even haystacks (and light) continue to be (iii)_____ today.

Blank (i)	Blank (ii)	Blank (iii)
A) reinventing	D) devotion	G) venerated
B) stabilizing	E) reverence	H) canonizing
C) consummate	F) praise	I) misunderstood

7. The mob's cruel conspiracy initially (i)_____ the villagers into a (ii)_____ refusal to fight. However, after a while the villagers' anger culminated, and they staged a

(iii)_____ destroying the mob and its convoluted, contentious efforts.

Blank (i)	Blank (ii)	Blank (iii)
A) confused	D) craven	G) unsurprising
B) upset	E) scornful	H) coup
C) cowed	F) sinister	I) cannon

8. His _____ disposition was without manners or elegance. In fact, his aberrant behavior left her brusquely offended.

- A) overbearing
- B) profound
- C) boorish
- D) caucus
- E) bourgeois

9. She ate very little and was similarly (i)_____ in purchasing clothing and jewelry. Instead, she preferred to live a (ii)_____ life.

Blank (i)	Blank (ii)
A) specialized	D) temperate
B) abstemious	E) gratifying
C) susceptible	F) expensive

10. While I should (i)_____ those whom I admire, I should not expect to fully realize their virtuous qualities. However, each time I (ii)_____, I will attempt to recommit myself to acting with (iii)_____.

Blank (i)	Blank (ii)	Blank (iii)
A) emulate	D) pivot	G) triviality
B) gravitate	E) diverge	H) implementation
C) impress	F) compete	I) propriety

RESEARCH **PREP.** GRE

www.research-prep.com

> Research**Prep**.GRE
>
> Text Completion Question Set #3
> Answers and Explanations

#1: The question was:

1. After describing the author as anything other than insignificant, the book review changed when describing the movie made about her work, which was_____.

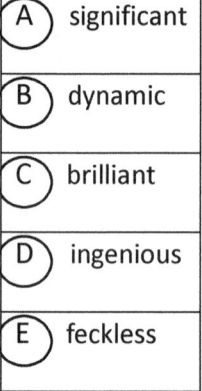

- (A) significant
- (B) dynamic
- (C) brilliant
- (D) ingenious
- (E) feckless

The correct answer is:

(E) feckless

The Verbal Reasoning and Analytical Writing Measures

RESEARCH PREP. GRE
www.research-prep.com

The answer choice vocabulary words and their synonyms are:

Answer Choice Vocabulary	Synonyms
Significant	Important, seminal, pivotal
Dynamic	Energized, having multiple capabilities
Brilliant	Ingenious, smart
Ingenious	Clever, surprisingly smart
Feckless	Ineffective, irresponsible

#2: The question was:

2. The bank created pamphlets explaining (i)_____ and (ii)_____ to help families create budgets and stick to them in the economic downturn.

Blank (i)	Blank (ii)
A) proxy	D) economy
B) wealth	E) frustration
C) frugality	F) fortitude

The correct answers are:

Blank (i):

C) frugality

Blank (ii):

D) economy

RESEARCH **PREP.** GRE

www.research-prep.com

The answer choice vocabulary words and their synonyms are:

Answer Choice Vocabulary	Synonyms
Proxy	Authorized agent for one or more actions
Wealth	Riches, overabundance
Frugality	Thriftiness
Economy	Efficiency, frugality
Frustration	Feeling thwarted, feeling defeated
Fortitude	Steadfastness, ability to withstand harm

#3: The question was:

3. The movie industry transitioned from silent films to "talkies" so long ago that many children (i)_____ do not (ii)_____ the (iii)_____ silent films.

Blank (i)	Blank (ii)	Blank (iii)
(A) omnisciently	(D) recall	(G) provincial
(B) contemporaneously	(E) rapport	(H) outmoded
(C) today	(F) query	(I) outspoken

The correct answers are:

Blank (i):

(C) today

|134|

The Verbal Reasoning and Analytical Writing Measures

Blank (ii):

(D) recall

Blank (iii):

(H) outmoded

The answer choice vocabulary words and their synonyms are:

Answer Choice Vocabulary	Synonyms
Omnisciently	All-knowing
Contemporaneously	At the same time, simultaneously (or nearly so)
Today	Current timeframe, the present, this day
Recall	Remember, recollect
Rapport	Emotionally connected, happy with one another
Query	Question
Provincial	From the countryside, unsophisticated
Outmoded	Old fashioned, out of date
Outspoken	Overt, communicative, forthright

#4: The question was:

4. During the world wars _____ were sometimes imprisoned for their refusal to become soldiers, but they would also serve in non-arms bearing capacities such as, serving as medical personnel.

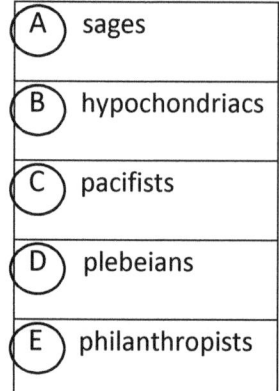

The correct answer is:

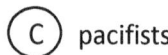

The answer choice vocabulary words and their synonyms are:

Answer Choice Vocabulary	Synonyms
Sages	People known for their wisdom
Hypochondriacs	Overly fearful of illness
Pacifists	Non-violent people, taking a political position against violence
Plebeians	Commoners
Philanthropists	Benefactors, those who do good acts

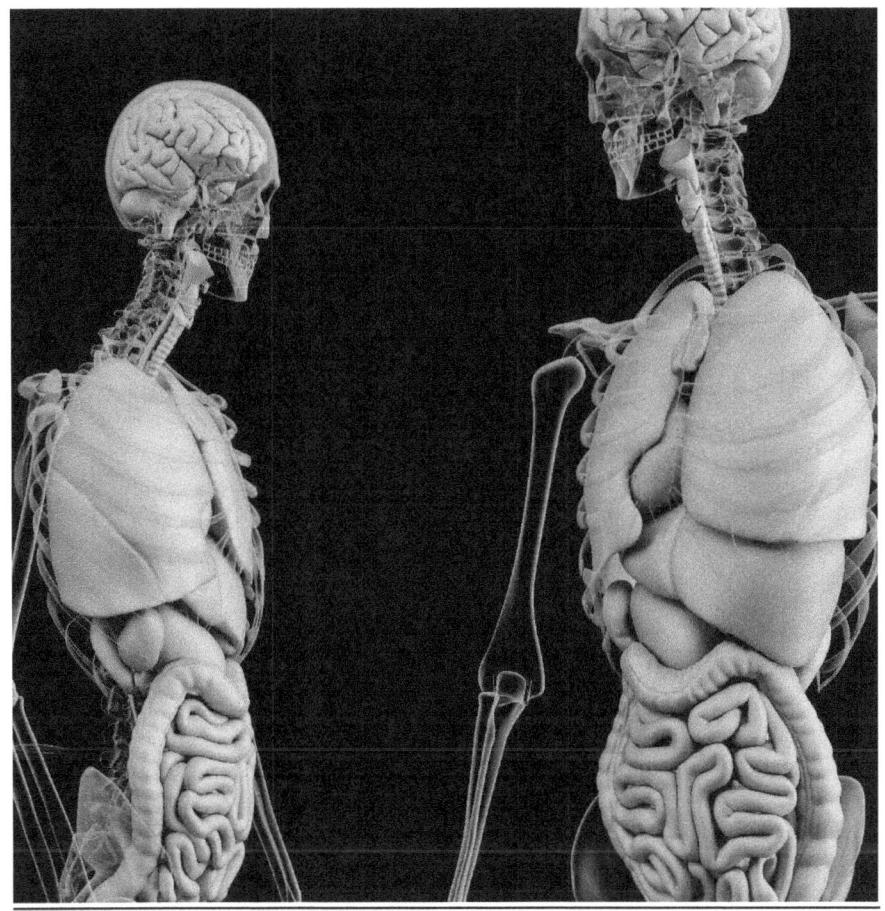

#5: The question was:

5. Walden pond was calm and placid, a place where Henry David Thoreau could likewise remain (i)_____ by leaving behind the insolent and (ii)_____ people who cause disruption in everyday life.

	Blank (i)		Blank (ii)
A	dauntless	D	impertinent
B	poignant	E	helpful
C	imperturbable	F	reverent

The correct answers are:

Blank (i):

C) imperturbable

Blank (ii):

D) impertinent

The answer choice vocabulary words and their synonyms are:

Answer Choice Vocabulary	Synonyms
Dauntless	Bold, lacking fear, cannot be deterred
Poignant	Keenly felt, emotionally touching, deeply moving
Imperturbable	Undisturbed, not aggravated, calm
Impertinent	Impudent, rude, insolent
Helpful	Assisting, provisional, giving
Reverent	Worship, respect without reservation, to venerate

#6: The question was:

6. Van Gogh's work displayed his (i)_____ artistic skill and heartfelt (ii)_____ which is why his paintings of even haystacks (and light) continue to be (iii)_____ today.

RESEARCH PREP. GRE
www.research-prep.com

	Blank (i)		Blank (ii)		Blank (iii)
A	reinventing	D	devotion	G	venerated
B	stabilizing	E	reverence	H	canonizing
C	consummate	F	praise	I	misunderstood

The correct answers are:

Blank (i):

(C) consummate

Blank (ii):

(D) devotion

Blank (iii):

(G) venerated

The answer choice vocabulary words and their synonyms are:

Answer Choice Vocabulary	Synonyms
Reinventing	Fully revise, completely change
Stabilizing	Support, make solid, prevent tipping
Consummate	Complete without deviation, flawless
Devotion	Diligently applying oneself, piety (devotion to God)
Reverence	Worship, respect without reservation, venerate

Praise	To communicate approval, speak well regarding
Venerated	Revered, idolized
Canonizing	Sanctify, consecrate
Misunderstood	Failed to comprehend

#7: The question was:

7. The mob's cruel conspiracy initially (i)_____ the villagers into a (ii)_____ refusal to fight. However, after a while the villagers' anger culminated, and they staged a (iii)_____, destroying the mob and its convoluted, contentious efforts.

Blank (i)	Blank (ii)	Blank (iii)
(A) confused	(D) craven	(G) unsurprising
(B) upset	(E) scornful	(H) coup
(C) cowed	(F) sinister	(I) cannon

The correct answers are:

Blank (i):

(C) cowed

Blank (ii):

(D) craven

Blank (iii):

(H) coup

The answer choice vocabulary words and their synonyms are:

Answer Choice Vocabulary	Synonyms
Confused	Trouble comprehending, not grasping
Upset	Sad, mad, negative emotions
Cowed	Intimidated, scared
Craven	Cowardly, fearful
Scornful	Look down on, wickedly undermine
Sinister	Evil, wicked
Unsurprising	Anticipated, known to be likely
Coup	Surprising attack, uprising
Cannon	Doctrine, important precepts

#8: The question was:

8. His _____ disposition was without manners or elegance. In fact, his aberrant behavior left her brusquely offended.

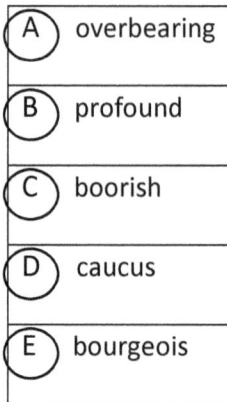

- A) overbearing
- B) profound
- C) boorish
- D) caucus
- E) bourgeois

RESEARCH PREP. GRE
www.research-prep.com

The correct answer is:

(C) boorish

The answer choice vocabulary words and their synonyms are:

Answer Choice Vocabulary	Synonyms
Overbearing	Arrogant, domineering, overly decisive for another
Profound	Deep, insightful
Boorish	Piggish, rude
Caucus	Party members' small group meeting
Bourgeois	Of the middle class; Selfish, materialistic in nature

#9: The question was:

9. She ate very little and was similarly (i)_____ in purchasing clothing and jewelry. Instead, she preferred to live a (ii)_____ life.

Blank (i)	Blank (ii)
(A) specialized	(D) temperate
(B) abstemious	(E) gratifying
(C) susceptible	(F) expensive

The Verbal Reasoning and Analytical Writing Measures

The correct answers are:

Blank (i):

(B) abstemious

Blank (ii):

(D) temperate

The answer choice vocabulary words and their synonyms are:

Answer Choice Vocabulary	Synonyms
Specialized	Pertaining to a unique field, an important portion, sophisticated
Abstemious	Sparing, temperate, without indulgence
Susceptible	Can be influenced, cannot withstand
Temperate	Having self-control, showing restraint; moderate temperature
Gratifying	Pleasing, pleasurable
Expensive	Costly

#10: The question was:

10. While I should (i)_____ those whom I admire, I should not expect to fully realize their virtuous qualities. However, each time I (ii)_____, I will attempt to recommit myself to acting with (iii)_____.

	Blank (i)		Blank (ii)		Blank (iii)
(A)	emulate	(D)	pivot	(G)	triviality
(B)	gravitate	(E)	diverge	(H)	implementation
(C)	impress	(F)	compete	(I)	propriety

The correct answers are:

Blank (i):

(A) emulate

Blank (ii):

(E) diverge

Blank (iii):

(I) propriety

The answer choice vocabulary words and their synonyms are:

Answer Choice Vocabulary	Synonyms
Emulate	Imitate, to strive to be like another
Gravitate	Move toward, become closer, not resist
Impress	Influence, awe
Pivot	Change directions while keeping one foot in place
Diverge	Move away from, go in another direction
Compete	Go up against in contest

Triviality	Unimportant, trifling, frivolous
Implementation	Put into action, to begin
Propriety	Having decorum, behaving with manners, conducting oneself properly

ResearchPrep.GRE

Text Completion Question Set #4

1. While the new student was smart, it was (i)_____ of her to challenge others' conclusions so early on. However, when her results were successful, the professors (ii)_____ the paper, despite the fact that it could also be looked at as good but mundane, rather than a (iii)_____ change in the field. Therefore, their discredit provided attention and strengthened others' views of her.

Blank (i)	Blank (ii)	Blank (iii)
(A) presumptuous	(D) confused	(G) caret
(B) baleful	(E) derided	(H) profound
(C) cajoling	(F) exhausted	(I) accredited

2. The (i)_____ of business seemed exciting and (ii)_____ all at once. But, he knew that the hard work would pay off, and his (iii)_____ sales would amount to considerable wealth.

	Blank (i)		Blank (ii)		Blank (iii)
A	exigencies	D	superfluous	G	aggregating
B	pariah	E	exacting	H	lucid
C	emergence	F	glib	I	elusive

3. Their (i)_____ communicatory friendship was quickly developing into (ii)_____, loving conversations. She felt their deepening affection was starting to show through the sensible facade.

	Blank (i)		Blank (ii)
A	prosaic	D	haughty
B	pompous	E	deferential
C	amicable	F	indolent

4. The costume designer's use of_____ outfits caused the fun play to be more fanciful and capricious than the last time the children came to see it!

A	altruistic
B	voluminous

C	cunning
D	whimsical
E	wry

5. The university soared in the rankings because of the presence of (i)_____ who (ii)_____ wrote well-researched, yet (iii)_____ texts that fostered research, culture, and creativity in the university community.

Blank (i)	Blank (ii)	Blank (iii)
A subordinates	D prodigiously	G morose
B sycophants	E querulously	H scintillating
C luminaries	F mockingly	I mundane

6. Propaganda has been used in communication through mass media to varying degrees of effectiveness. Today it seems that people are less (i)_____ propaganda then years ago.

A	aware of
B	influenced by
C	impressed by

D	irked by
E	scornful of

7. In Alfred Hitchcock's films, displays of violence were often downplayed because their (i)_____ nature was so shocking that it would have been a (ii)_____ over display, rather than a (iii)_____ scene in a suspenseful film.

Blank (i)	Blank (ii)	Blank (iii)
A) morbid	D) divergent	G) pivotal
B) punctilious	E) fatuous	H) doctrinaire
C) extrinsic	F) grotesque	I) ebullient

8. Charlotte Brontë may be a lesser-known author than her sister Emily Brontë, but her literary work *Jane Eyre* cannot be (i)_____ too highly. It is (ii)_____ and significant.

Blank (i)	Blank (ii)
A) extolled	D) insightful
B) acknowledged	E) abstemious

| C | beseeched | F | imperious |

9. By mile sixteen, the task of finishing her first marathon seemed (i)_____, but she (ii)_____ kept running, and by mile twenty-four, with just over two miles to go, she knew that because of the (iii)_____ of the finish line, her goal was achievable!

Blank (i)	Blank (ii)	Blank (iii)
A) poignant	D) surreptitiously	G) temerity
B) insurmountable	E) tacitly	H) viability
C) histrionic	F) pragmatically	I) proximity

10. (i)_____ people and tribes in various areas have at times performed sacrifices, seeking to (ii)_____ the gods.

Blank (i)	Blank (ii)
A) ubiquitous	D) recidivism
B) indigenous	E) propitiate
C) recalcitrant	F) umbrage

RESEARCH **PREP.** GRE

www.research-prep.com

Research**Prep.**GRE

Text Completion Question Set #4

Answers and Explanations

#1: The question was:

1. While the new student was smart, it was (i)_____ of her to challenge others' conclusions so early on. However, when her results were successful, the professors (ii)_____ the paper, despite the fact that it could also be looked at as good but mundane, rather than a (iii)_____ change in the field. Therefore, their discredit provided attention and strengthened others' views of her.

Blank (i)	Blank (ii)	Blank (iii)
A) presumptuous	D) confused	G) caret
B) baleful	E) derided	H) profound
C) cajoling	F) exhausted	I) accredited

The correct answers are:

Blank (i):

(A) presumptuous

Blank (ii):

(E) derided

Blank (iii):

(H) profound

The answer choice vocabulary words and their synonyms are:

Answer Choice Vocabulary	Synonyms
Presumptuous	Arrogant, pretentious
Baleful	Sinister, threatening
Cajoling	Coaxing, convincing
Confused	Mixed up, disoriented, bewildered, puzzled
Derided	Ridiculed, berated
Exhausted	Extremely tired; used up (finite resources)
Caret	Reference mark
Profound	Important, pivotal, significant
Accredited	Having authorization from a controlling entity (a school term); authorized

#2: The question was:

2. The (i)_____ of business seemed exciting and (ii)_____ all at once. But, he knew that the hard work would pay off, and his (iii)_____ sales would amount to considerable wealth.

	Blank (i)		Blank (ii)		Blank (iii)
A	exigencies	D	superfluous	G	aggregating
B	pariah	E	exacting	H	lucid
C	emergence	F	glib	I	elusive

The correct answers are:

Blank (i):

(A) exigencies

Blank (ii):

(E) exacting

Blank (iii):

(G) aggregating

The answer choice vocabulary words and their synonyms are:

Answer Choice Vocabulary	Synonyms
Exigencies	Demands, urgencies, pressing needs
Pariah	Socially ostracized person, outcast
Emergence	Coming out to be seen
Superfluous	Additional and unnecessary, excessive
Exacting	Exceedingly demanding, tediously requiring

Glib	Quick fluency, short and concise speech, quick witty remarks
Aggregating	Accumulating, adding more
Lucid	Clear, understandable
Elusive	Evasive, out of reach

#3: The question was:

3. Their (i)_____ communicatory friendship was quickly developing into (ii)_____, loving conversations. She felt their deepening affection was starting to show through the sensible facade.

Blank (i)	Blank (ii)
(A) prosaic	(D) haughty
(B) pompous	(E) deferential
(C) amicable	(F) indolent

The correct answers are:

Blank (i):

(C) amicable

Blank (ii):

(E) deferential

RESEARCH **PREP.** GRE

www.research-prep.com

The answer choice vocabulary words and their synonyms are:

Answer Choice Vocabulary	Synonyms
Prosaic	Unimaginative, boring, not creative
Pompous	Self-involved, haughty, full of oneself
Amicable	Polite, friendly
Haughty	Arrogant, pompous
Deferential	Kindly providing agreement, courtesy with respect or sweetness
Indolent	Lazy

#4: The question was:

4. The costume designer's use of _____ outfits caused the fun play to be more fanciful and capricious than the last time the children came to see it!

- (A) altruistic
- (B) voluminous
- (C) cunning
- (D) whimsical
- (E) wry

The correct answer is:

(D) whimsical

|156|

The Verbal Reasoning and Analytical Writing Measures

The answer choice vocabulary words and their synonyms are:

Answer Choice Vocabulary	Synonyms
Altruistic	Generous and not concerned with oneself, a positive outlook
Voluminous	Large, big
Cunning	Keen sense of a situation
Whimsical	Fanciful, playful, capricious
Wry	Humorous but biting or dry, a humorous twist

RESEARCH **PREP.** GRE

www.research-prep.com

#5: The question was:

5. The university soared in the rankings because of the presence of (i)_____ who (ii)_____ wrote well-researched, yet (iii)_____ texts which fostered research, culture, and creativity in the university community.

Blank (i)	Blank (ii)	Blank (iii)
(A) subordinates	(D) prodigiously	(G) morose
(B) sycophants	(E) querulously	(H) scintillating
(C) luminaries	(F) mockingly	(I) mundane

The correct answers are:

Blank (i):

(C) luminaries

Blank (ii):

(D) prodigiously

Blank (iii):

(H) scintillating

The answer choice vocabulary words and their synonyms are:

Answer Choice Vocabulary	Synonyms
Subordinates	Lower ranking, inferior position
Sycophants	Those who cater to another, flatterers, "yes men"
Luminaries	Notables, leaders, celebrities
Prodigiously	Large volume, significant amount
Querulously	Argumentatively
Mockingly	Imitate, ridicule by mimicking
Morose	Sullen, grumpy
Scintillating	Sparking, engaging
Mundane	Worldly (not-spiritual), ordinary

#6: The question was:

6. Propaganda has been used in communication through mass media to varying degrees of effectiveness. Today it seems that people are less (i)_____ propaganda than years ago.

- A) aware of
- B) influenced by
- C) impressed by
- D) irked by
- E) scornful of

RESEARCH **PREP.** GRE
www.research-prep.com

The correct answer is:

(B) influenced by

The answer choice vocabulary words and their synonyms are:

Answer Choice Vocabulary	Synonyms
Aware of	Noticing
Influenced by	To make decisions based on
Impressed by	Finding it important and significant
Irked by	Angered by, annoyed by
Scornful of	Angry with, to deride

#7: The question was:

7. In Alfred Hitchcock's films, displays of violence were often downplayed because their (i)_____ nature was so shocking that it would have been a (ii)_____ over display, rather than a (iii)_____ scene in a suspenseful film.

Blank (i)	Blank (ii)	Blank (iii)
(A) morbid	(D) divergent	(G) pivotal
(B) punctilious	(E) fatuous	(H) doctrinaire
(C) extrinsic	(F) grotesque	(I) ebullient

The Verbal Reasoning and Analytical Writing Measures

The correct answers are:

Blank (i):

(A) morbid

Blank (ii):

(F) grotesque

Blank (iii):

(G) pivotal

The answer choice vocabulary words and their synonyms are:

Answer Choice Vocabulary	Synonyms
Morbid	Dark thoughts, unwholesome ideas
Punctilious	Overly attentive to detail, fastidious
Extrinsic	External; non-essential
Divergent	Differing, varied
Fatuous	Foolish and self-important
Grotesque	Hideous, disgusting
Pivotal	Critical, important
Doctrinaire	Adhering to doctrine, sticking to orthodox thought
Ebullient	Enthusiastic, bubbling over, exuberant

#8: The question was:

8. Charlotte Brontë may be a lesser-known author than her sister Emily Brontë, but her literary work *Jane Eyre* cannot be (i)_____ too highly. It is (ii)_____ and significant.

Blank (i)	Blank (ii)
(A) extolled	(D) insightful
(B) acknowledged	(E) abstemious
(C) beseeched	(F) imperious

The correct answers are:

Blank (i):

(A) extolled

Blank (ii):

(D) insightful

The answer choice vocabulary words and their synonyms are:

Answer Choice Vocabulary	Synonyms
Extolled	Praised
Acknowledged	Confirmed, recognized, admitted
Beseeched	Pleaded, requested, begged
Insightful	Discerning, understanding, perceptive
Abstemious	Sparing, without indulging
Imperious	Haughty

#9: The question was:

9. By mile sixteen the task of finishing her first marathon seemed (i)_____, but she (ii)_____ kept running, and by mile twenty-four, with just over two miles to go, she knew that because of the (iii)_____ of the finish line, her goal was achievable!

Blank (i)	Blank (ii)	Blank (iii)
(A) poignant	(D) surreptitiously	(G) temerity

| B | insurmountable | E | tacitly | H | viability |
| C | histrionic | F | pragmatically | I | proximity |

The correct answers are:

Blank (i):

(B) insurmountable

Blank (ii):

(F) pragmatically

Blank (iii):

(I) proximity

The answer choice vocabulary words and their synonyms are:

Answer Choice Vocabulary	Synonyms
Poignant	Emotionally moving, keenly felt
Insurmountable	Overwhelming, impossible, insufferable
Histrionic	Theatrical
Surreptitiously	Secretly, furtively
Tacitly	Understood but not communicated
Pragmatically	Practically (rather than idealistically)
Temerity	Boldness
Viability	Workable, maintainable
Proximity	Closeness, whereabouts, nearness

#10: The question was:

10. (i)_____ people and tribes in various areas have at times performed sacrifices, seeking to (ii)_____ the gods.

Blank (i)	Blank (ii)
(A) ubiquitous	(D) recidivism

(B) indigenous	(E) propitiate
(C) recalcitrant	(F) umbrage

The correct answers are:

Blank (i):

(B) indigenous

Blank (ii):

(E) propitiate

The answer choice vocabulary words and their synonyms are:

Answer Choice Vocabulary	Synonyms
Ubiquitous	Omnipresent, all around, universal
Indigenous	Native to a place, originating in the area
Recalcitrant	Obstinate, resistant, stubborn
Recidivism	Repeatedly committing crimes
Propitiate	Appease, mollify, diminish the anger of
Umbrage	Resentment

CHAPTER #3

THE VERBAL REASONING MEASURE

Reading Comprehension Questions

Reading Comprehension Questions

On the GRE, reading comprehension questions test your ability to read and understand difficult (and sometimes exceedingly difficult) texts. GRE reading comprehension passages are presented on the test in varied lengths. They are often parts of larger intellectual texts that have been removed from their original context and modified into test passages.

Expect to see passages from scholarly journals, government documents, and even literature. Before you are tested on the passages, they are sometimes significantly changed by test editors. Therefore, expect that they may not read fluidly. The passage will always exclude the larger context in which it was originally written. Sometimes, it seems jarring to jump into a passage on the GRE because you begin at the heart of the issue (as identified to test your reading comprehension) without context or introduction. Test-makers also add complex grammar and change vocabulary used in the passages before you are tested on them.

To tackle a reading comprehension passage:

First, glance at the number of questions that relate to that passage. Notably, sometimes a long passage has only one question related to it. Do not devote a great deal of time to that passage. If there are only one or two questions for a lengthy passage, then read the question prompts (but not the answer choices) before reading the passage.

Second, read the passage fully. Aim to move quickly, but slowly enough to absorb the meaning from the text. Spend more time reading when several questions relate to that passage. Read carefully enough to comprehend what you are reading; this means that you must absorb the meaning of the text.

Third, read each question and answer them in order. You will likely have to look back at the text to answer each question. Review the passage for that specific answer and then answer the question based on what you have found.

Fourth, do not leave any blank answers. If you must, make an "educated guess" by eliminating as many answer choices as possible and then guessing from the few left that might be right. If you guess, mark that question for your review at the end of the test, and return to those choices if you have time. When moving through the test the first time, guess when you have to; do not leave any blank answers.

When considering time, remember that correct answers to the questions always come from the passages. When reading, allow yourself to slow down and absorb the meaning of the passage you are reading. Just read and absorb; while moving quickly is important, comprehending the passage is crucial to answering every question on the test. Move only as quickly as you can while maintaining your ability to absorb and understand the text.

Do not cloud your mind with your own questions (What is the tone? Why does the author transition here? What is the author trying to do when he writes it in this way?) Superfluous mental questioning is not needed.

Do not leave reading comprehension questions unanswered as you move through the test. Pick an answer and guess. Returning to answer these questions later is exceedingly difficult because you will have read other passages in the interim. The passages can blur together in your mind after reading several of them. You will likely have to re-read a large part of the passage later to recollect it and find a new answer. Therefore, answer each question in order, even if it is just an "educated guess" achieved by eliminating choices that you can distinguish as wrong. You can press the "mark" button to flag the question, then you will be able to quickly return to it at the end of the entire section if you end up finishing early. Just make sure that you select an answer at the time you initially read the passage. Most likely, you will not have time to return to the passage and re-familiarize yourself with it. The best time to answer is while the passage is still fresh in your mind the first time you work through the test.

Finally, follow the instructions for the specific question. If the instructions tell you that you may select more than one answer choice, then select all correct choices. Questions with instructions to select as many correct choices as you find are most often also shown by square boxes around each answer choice. So, if you see squares, then look at the directions for that question because you likely need to consider selecting several answer choices. These often look like this:

> For this question, consider each answer choice separately and choose all correct answer choices.

1. The question will be written here; remember to select all correct

   - [A] answer choices.
   - [B] answer choices.
   - [C] answer choices.

Some questions may ask you to underline a sentence (mechanically, this is very easy on the computer based GRE). You may also be asked to review a highlighted portion of a passage. Just

RESEARCH PREP. GRE
www.research-prep.com

follow the specific instructions, and try to choose the correct answer for each question.

Most questions will request that you select a single answer, and these most often have circles around the answer choices. Just check the instructions if needed.

1. The question will be written here; remember to select one correct
   - (A) answer choice.
   - (B) no additional answer choices.
   - (C) no additional answer choices.
   - (D) no additional answer choices.
   - (E) no additional answer choices.

Also consider the "best of the best" and the "best of the bad." On the GRE, sometimes two or more answer choices work well. You must choose the better of the two good choices. Research Prep. calls this the "best of the best" dilemma. Remember, you may have two or more great choices -- try to pick the best one. This also works the other way: you may have all bad answer choices. Not one is good enough to be the answer to the question. Research Prep. calls this the problem of the "best of the bad." When all of the answer choices are bad ones, pick the best of the bad choices.

To reiterate the strategy, just read to quickly absorb the meaning as you move through the passage. Then, answer the questions in order. Read each question and its answer choices and go back to the passage as needed to identify your answer. Expect to return to the passage after you read each question to find your answer. Follow any special instructions (such as those telling you to select all correct answer choices for that question or to underline the sentence containing your answer). Always pick your best answer and move forward to the next question. If you are uncertain exclude as many wrong answers as you can and guess. Mark guesses to review at the end if there is time.

ResearchPrep.GRE

Reading Comprehension Passage #1
Question Set

'The Cowboy Artist' Charles Merion Russell was born in 1864 in St. Louis, Missouri. At the time, the 'Gateway to the West' was crowded with fur traders and bustling with steamboat traffic. William Brent, Russell's great-uncle, was the first Caucasian settler of the area of Colorado. Russell traveled west and became renowned for his paintings of cowboys and Native American Indians on the western frontier. Russell's work evokes the excitement of life in a frontier town *'Utica (A Quiet Day in Utica),'* 1907 (oil on canvas); the significance and austerity of a lone Native American scout *'The Scout,'* 1907 (pencil, watercolor and gouache on paper); the real work of cowboys *'When Cowboys Get in Trouble (The Mad Cow),'* 1899 (oil on canvas); and clashing of Native American tribes *'When Blackfeet and Sioux Meet,'* 1908 (oil on canvas). Russell even ventured close enough to paint sweet depictions of Native American women peacefully bathing children, *'Three Generations,'* 1897 (oil on canvas).

Russell's beautiful and startling depictions of this time of transition of the western frontier were perfectly timed. By the time Russell died, the frontier had transitioned from the 'Old West' frontier towns, Native American Indian homelands, buffalo hunts, and cowboys' cattle drives, to settlement; ranches, farming, the control of the U.S. military, and the popularity of railroads, had subdued the 'Great Plains.'

1. The author's intended audience for this passage is most likely comprised of --
(A) historical-fiction readers.
(B) science museum visitors.
(C) art history students.
(D) fourth grade students.
(E) social science professors.

2. The author's attitude toward Russell's dedication to his artwork, as shown by the highlighted text, can best be described as --
(A) categorical.
(B) irreverent.
(C) affiable.
(D) clandestine.
(E) admiring.

3. Select the sentence in the second paragraph that best supports the claim of the author that Russell's artwork was 'perfectly timed.'

4. From the passage, it can be inferred that –
(A) Russell also painted steamboats.
(B) battles at times occurred between Native American tribes, not only between Native Americans and Caucasians.

(C) Native Americans forbade Russell, a Caucasian, from painting them.

(D) Russell was a poor artist.

(E) the 'Gateway to the West,' the 'Old West,' and the 'Great Plains' are all interchangeable terms.

RESEARCH **PREP.** GRE

www.research-prep.com

Research**Prep.**GRE

Reading Comprehension Passage #1
Answers and Explanations

The passage was:

    'The Cowboy Artist,' Charles Merion Russell was born in 1864 in St. Louis, Missouri. At the time, the 'Gateway to the West' was crowded with fur traders and bustling with steamboat traffic. William Brent, Russell's great-uncle, was the first Caucasian settler of the area of Colorado. Russell traveled west and became renowned for his paintings of cowboys and Native American Indians on the western frontier. Russell's work evokes the excitement of life in a frontier town *'Utica (A Quiet Day in Utica),'* 1907 (oil on canvas); the significance and austerity of a lone Native American scout *'The Scout,'* 1907 (pencil, watercolor, and gouache on paper); the real work of cowboys *'When Cowboys Get in Trouble (The Mad Cow),'* 1899 (oil on canvas); and clashing of Native American tribes *'When Blackfeet and Sioux Meet,'* 1908 (oil on canvas). ==Russell even ventured close enough to paint sweet depictions of Native American women peacefully bathing children, *'Three Generations,'* 1897 (oil on canvas).==

    Russell's beautiful and startling depictions of this time of transition of the western frontier were perfectly timed. <u>By the time Russell died, the frontier had transitioned from the 'Old West' frontier towns, Native American Indian homelands, buffalo hunts, and cowboys' cattle drives, to settlement; ranches, farming, the</u>

control of the U.S. military, and the popularity of railroads, had subdued the 'Great Plains.'

#1: The question was:

1. The author's intended audience for this passage is most likely comprised of --
(A) historical-fiction readers.
(B) science museum visitors.
(C) art history students.
(D) fourth grade students.
(E) social science professors.

The correct answer is:
(C) art history students.

This is why:
This question asks you to infer the author's intended audience from the information contained in the passage.
- **Choice C** is correct because the passage discusses an artist and his artwork, within a historical context.
- **Choice A** is incorrect because the passage is non-fiction.
- **Choice B** is incorrect because the focus of the passage is artwork, rather than science.
- **Choice D** is incorrect because the passage does not appear to target elementary school students as the readers; it is too advanced for them.

- **Choice E** is incorrect because the passage is not about social science. It is about a depiction of a turbulent time in human history through artwork.

#2: The question was:

2. The author's attitude toward Russell's dedication to his artwork, as shown by the highlighted text, can best be described as --

A) categorical.
B) irreverent.
C) affiable.
D) clandestine.
E) admiring.

The correct answer is:
E) admiring.

This is why:
- **Choice E** is correct because the author seems to admire Russell's dedication when she writes, Russell "even ventured close enough to paint sweet depictions…"
- **Choice A** is incorrect because *categorical* means to be categorized without any exceptions. The author is fully positive about Russell's dedication, but A is still not the best choice because it does not convey the correct tone (the author's perspective and attitude), which are better described by Choice E, admiring.

- **Choice B** is incorrect because *irreverent* means disrespectful or without propriety. This is not the author's attitude toward Russell's dedication.
- **Choice C** is incorrect because *affable* means warm, easygoing, friendly, and approachable, but it is still not a better description then Choice E.
- **Choice D** is incorrect because *clandestine* means secret. While the women and children depicted may appear to be bathing in secret, the author's attitude toward Russell's dedication to his artwork is not itself 'secret.'

#3: The question was:

3. Select the sentence in the second paragraph which best supports the claim of the author that Russell's artwork was 'perfectly timed.'

The correct answer is:
This is the correct sentence to underline on the GRE:

"By the time Russell died, the frontier had transitioned from the 'Old West' frontier towns, Native American Indian homelands, buffalo hunts, and cowboys' cattle drives, to settlement; ranches, farming, the control of the U.S. military, and the popularity of railroads, had subdued the 'Great Plains.'"

This is the correct answer because it provides support for the author's claim, which is made in the earlier sentence. The sentence making the claim of perfect timing itself is not the support but the claim. So the sentence preceding this one is an incorrect answer.

#4: The question was:

4. From the passage, it can be inferred that —

(A) Russell also painted steamboats.

(B) battles at times occurred between Native American tribes, not only between Native Americans and Caucasians.

(C) Native Americans forbade Russell, a Caucasian, from painting them.

(D) Russell was a poor artist.

(E) the 'Gateway to the West,' the 'Old West,' and the 'Great Plains' are all interchangeable terms.

The correct answer is:
(B) battles at times occurred between Native American tribes, not only between Native Americans and Caucasians.

This is why:
- **Choice B** is correct because the passage describes and lists a painting title stating, "…and clashing of Native American tribes '*When Blackfeet and Sioux Meet*,' 1908 (oil on canvas)." This is just before the highlighted sentence.
- **Choice A** is incorrect because the passage states that "Russell traveled west and became renowned for his paintings of cowboys and Native American Indians on the western frontier." The passage only states that Russell grew up in St. Louis, which was bustling with steamboats. Then he moved west to paint. It does not state that he painted steamboats.
- **Choice C** is incorrect because it appears from the passage that Russell may have been invited by Native Americans at times. However, it also appears that Russell is likely Caucasian (based on his name and the reference to his great uncle, a Caucasian settler).
- **Choice D** is incorrect because the passage says Russell was "…renowned for his paintings of cowboys and Native American Indians on the western frontier." It does not say whether he was poor, but still a 'renowned' artist. Without any specific information about money, use of the term 'renowned' does not address the issue of poverty.
- **Choice E** is incorrect because while the author appears to use 'Old West,' and 'Great Plains' synonymously, she uses

'Gateway to the West' to refer to St. Louis and its bustling steamboat traffic.

ResearchPrep.GRE

Reading Comprehension Passage #2
Question Set

In his book <u>The Structure of Scientific Revolutions,</u> Thomas Kuhn described scientific change in a new way. Kuhn's theory of scientific behavior and scientific change is designed around a paradigm. According to Kuhn, "pre-paradigm" science is science practiced before the development of a paradigm. For example, this state might exist in a new field. The work done during "pre-paradigm" science is neither as organized nor as effective as work done in the paradigm. A paradigm develops when an impressive model of work occurs which serves as an exemplar for the work of other scientists. Around this excellent example, a field develops consistent methods for obtaining and analyzing data, developing theories, and performing all other facets of work within a field. Scientific work becomes organized within the paradigm.

Overtime, a paradigm can falter when anomalies start to accumulate and scientists' faith in the fundamental precepts of their paradigm is shaken. When too many anomalies accrue and too many scientists question the soundness of the fundamental principles upon which the paradigm is based, "crisis" occurs. If a new contending paradigm is available and the field is in "crisis," a "scientific revolution" can occur. If it does, the old paradigm is rejected and replaced with a new accepted paradigm. This "scientific revolution" is a momentous change within the field.

For this question, consider each answer choice separately and choose all correct answer choices.

5. Which statements can be logically inferred as true based on the passage?

A   Thomas Kuhn thought of scientific change differently than others who studied it.

B   At times, scientists model their work methods after other scientists, and this is an effective way for scientists to approach their work, according to Kuhn.

C   A "scientific revolution" will always occur if a scientist finds an anomaly within the precept of a paradigm.

6. The author of the passage would likely believe which of the situations presented in the answer choices is the most analogous to Kuhn's view of a "scientific revolution," as described in the highlighted sentence?

A) A change of the town's mayor based on a popular vote.

B) A slow revision of a paper by its author.

C) A person changing overtime as he grows up and matures.

D) A momentary decision and a later change of plans.

F) A monumental change of our approach to an important issue.

7. It can be inferred that the author of the passage thinks that Thomas Kuhn would agree with which one of these statements?

(A) Scientific paradigms are lasting and irreplacable.

(B) Paradigms do not falter.

(C) Pre-paradigm science is somewhat disorganized when compared to science within a paradigm.

(D) A paradigm cannot be rejected.

(E) A scientific field is never actually considered to be "in crisis."

8. From the passage, we can infer that the author would agree with all of these statements, EXCEPT –

(A) Kuhn described scientific behavior.

(B) Kuhn described scientific change.

(C) It is a benefit for science to be well organized and follow consistent methods.

(D) Scientists' beliefs in the value of certain scientific precepts can change overtime.

(E) New scientific fields cannot be created anymore.

ResearchPrep.GRE

Reading Comprehension Passage #2
Answers and Explanations

The passage was:

In his book <u>The Structure of Scientific Revolutions,</u> Thomas Kuhn described scientific change in a new way. Kuhn's theory of scientific behavior and scientific change is designed around a paradigm. According to Kuhn, "pre-paradigm" science is science practiced before the development of a paradigm. For example, this state might exist in a new field. The work done during "pre-paradigm" science is neither as organized nor as effective as work done in the paradigm. A paradigm develops when an impressive model of work occurs which serves as an exemplar for the work of other scientists. Around this excellent example, a field develops consistent methods for obtaining and analyzing data, developing theories, and performing all other facets of work within a field. Scientific work becomes organized within the paradigm.

Overtime, a paradigm can falter when anomalies start to accumulate and scientists' faith in the fundamental precepts of their paradigm is shaken. When too many anomalies accrue and too many scientists question the soundness of the fundamental principles upon which the paradigm is based, "crisis" occurs. If a new contending paradigm is available and the field is in "crisis," a "scientific revolution" can occur. If it does, the old paradigm is rejected and replaced with a new accepted paradigm. This "scientific revolution" is a momentous change within the field.

RESEARCH **PREP.** GRE
www.research-prep.com

#5: The question was:

> For this question, consider each answer choice separately and choose all correct answer choices.

5. Which statements can be logically inferred as true based on the passage?

| A | Thomas Kuhn thought of scientific change differently than others who studied it.

| B | At times, scientists model their work methods after other scientists, and this is an effective way for scientists to approach their work, according to Kuhn.

| C | A "scientific revolution" will always occur if a scientist finds an anomaly within the precept of a paradigm.

The correct answers are:

| A | Thomas Kuhn thought of scientific change differently than others who studied it.

| B | At times, scientists model their work methods after other scientists, and this is an effective way for scientists to approach their work, according to Kuhn.

This is why:
First, remember that the instructions were to consider each answer choice separately and **choose all correct** answer choices.
- **Choice A** is correct because the passage states "...Kuhn described scientific change in a new way." From this we can

|188|

logically infer that Kuhn also thought about scientific change in a new way, and therefore, differently from others who studied it.
- **Choice B** is also correct based on the following sentences: "A paradigm develops when an impressive model of work occurs which serves as an exemplar for the work of other scientists. Around this excellent example, a field develops consistent methods for obtaining and analyzing data, developing theories, and performing all other facets of work within a field. Scientific work becomes organized within the paradigm." These sentences tell us that a scientist's work serves as a model or an example for other scientists' work and its effective organization within a field.
- **Choice C** is incorrect because it cannot be inferred that one anomaly found by one scientist will always cause a "scientific revolution." The passage states that "[w]hen too many anomalies accrue and too many scientists question…" This means that we cannot infer that one scientist and one anomaly are enough.

#6: The question was:

6. The author of the passage would likely believe which of the situations presented in the answer choices is the most analogous to Kuhn's view of a "scientific revolution" as described in the highlighted sentence?

(A) A change of the town's mayor based on a popular vote.

(B) A slow revision of a paper by its author.

(C) A person changing overtime as he grows up and matures.

(D) A momentary decision and a later change of plans.

(E) A monumental change of our approach to an important issue.

The correct answer is:
(E) A monumental change of our approach to an important issue.

This is why:
- **Choice E** is correct because it describes a "monumental change," which is the most similar to the highlighted sentence that calls a scientific revolution a "momentous change." Both monumental and momentous describe important changes.
- **None of the other answer choices** describe a large, important change as well as answer choice E.

#7: The question was:

7. It can be inferred that the author of the passage thinks that Thomas Kuhn would agree with which one of these statements?
(A) Scientific paradigms are lasting and irreplacable.
(B) Paradigms do not falter.
(C) Pre-paradigm science is somewhat disorganized when compared to science within a paradigm.
(D) A paradigm cannot be rejected.
(E) A scientific field is never actually considered to be "in crisis."

The correct answer is:
(C) Pre-paradigm science is somewhat disorganized when compared to science within a paradigm.

This is why:
- **Choice C** is correct because the first paragraph states that pre-paradigm science is not as organized as work done within the paradigm ("The work done during 'pre-paradigm' science is neither as organized nor as effective as work done in the paradigm.") It also states that the paradigm organizes the work ("Scientific work becomes organized within the paradigm.")
- **Choice A** is incorrect because the passage says that at times a paradigm is "replaced with a new accepted paradigm."
- **Choice B** is incorrect because the passage states that "Overtime, a paradigm can falter when anomalies start to accumulate and scientists' faith in the fundamental precepts of their paradigm is shaken."
- **Choice D** is incorrect because the passage states that at times, "...the old paradigm is rejected..."
- **Choice E** is incorrect because the passage states that "[i]f a new contending paradigm is available and the field is in 'crisis,' a 'scientific revolution' can occur." This shows that there are times when "the field is in 'crisis'" according to the passage.

#8: The question was:

8. From the passage, we can infer that the author would agree with all of these statements, EXCEPT –

(A) Kuhn described scientific behavior.

(B) Kuhn described scientific change.

(C) It is a benefit for science to be well organized and follow consistent methods.

(D) Scientists' beliefs in the value of certain scientific precepts can change overtime.

(E) New scientific fields cannot be created anymore.

The correct answer is:
(E) New scientific fields cannot be created anymore.

This is why:
- **Choice E** is correct because the author agrees with answer choices A, B, C, and D, as shown by the text.
- **Choice A** is incorrect because the author agrees with it as shown when she writes: "…Kuhn described scientific change in a new way. Kuhn's theory of scientific behavior…"
- **Choice B** is incorrect because the author agrees with it as shown when she writes: "In his book The Structure of Scientific Revolutions, Thomas Kuhn described scientific change in a new way."
- **Choice C** is incorrect because the author agrees with it as shown when she writes: "Around this **excellent example** …. Scientific **work becomes organized** within the paradigm."
- **Choice D** is incorrect because the author agrees with it as shown when she writes: "…**scientists' faith in the fundamental precepts** of their paradigm is shaken."

> Research**Prep**.GRE
>
> Reading Comprehension Passage #3
> # Question Set

Plaintiff Jack Hill asserts his only exposure to asbestos occurred while working as a well installer and union carpenter. Plaintiff testified that he was exposed to asbestos contained in wells while he worked as a well installer with his sister. T1:2-3:4. Relevant transcript portions, designated by "T1" are contained in Exhibit B, which was previously filed with the Court under the appropriate index number (and is therefore not attached hereto). Plaintiff occasionally installed wells with his sister between approximately 1952 and 1958 ("every once in a blue moon"). T1:2-3:4. Between 1958 and 1962, Plaintiff worked full time with his sister installing wells. T1:2-3:4. They operated a well installation company named Jack & Jill Wells. T1:2-3:4. Plaintiff installed wells outside of residential homes and commercial buildings in Manhattan, Long Island, and Brooklyn. T1:2-3:4. Plaintiff could not recall any specific location where he installed wells and could not recall the names of any of his co-workers, other than his sister, plaintiff Jill Hill. T1:2-3:4.

9. The author's use of the Jack and Jill reference can best be described as invoking –
(A) levity.
(B) ignominy.
(C) hubris.
(D) lethargy.

E) fanaticism.

10. Select the sentence in the passage that suggests that Jack Hill is unable to remember some specifics about his career.

For this question, consider each answer choice separately and choose all correct answer choices.

11. Which of these statements can be inferred from the passage?

A   Jack and Jill installed some wells and fountains inside of buildings.

B   Jack and Jill worked together more often once they went into business together.

C   Jill was probably also exposed to asbestos.

For this question, consider each answer choice separately and choose all correct answer choices.

12. Which of the following is needed by Plaintiffs Jack and Jill Hill to strengthen their claim or argument and win this lawsuit in court?

A   A delineated argument explaining how the exposure to asbestos caused them harm.

B   Specific opponents who caused the harm, whom Jack and Jill will sue for money.

C   Nothing, Jack and Jill are ready.

> Research**Prep**.GRE
>
> Reading Comprehension Passage #3
> ## Answers and Explanations

The passage was:

Plaintiff Jack Hill asserts his only exposure to asbestos occurred while working as a well installer and union carpenter. Plaintiff testified that he was exposed to asbestos contained in wells while he worked as a well installer with his sister. T1:2-3:4. Relevant transcript portions, designated by "T1" are contained in Exhibit B, which was previously filed with the Court under the appropriate index number (and is therefore not attached hereto). Plaintiff occasionally installed wells with his sister between approximately 1952 and 1958 ("every once in a blue moon"). T1:2-3:4. Between 1958 and 1962, Plaintiff worked full time with his sister installing wells. T1:2-3:4. They operated a well installation company named Jack & Jill Wells. T1:2-3:4. Plaintiff installed wells outside of residential homes and commercial buildings in Manhattan, Long Island, and Brooklyn. T1:2-3:4. <u>Plaintiff could not recall any specific location where he installed wells and could not recall the names of any of his co-workers, other than his sister, plaintiff Jill Hill.</u> T1:2-3:4.

#9: The question was:

9. The author's use of the Jack and Jill reference can best be described as invoking –
(A) levity.

(B) ignominy.
(C) hubris.
(D) lethargy.
(E) fanaticism.

The correct answer is:
(A) levity.

This is why:
- **Choice A** is correct because *levity* means humor or flippancy. Of the answer choices, this must be the correct answer based on the meanings of each potential choice.
- **Choice B** is incorrect because *ignominy* means disgrace or shame.
- **Choice C** is incorrect because *hubris* means arrogance or conceit.
- **Choice D** is incorrect because *lethargy* means tiredness or drowsiness.
- **Choice E** is incorrect because *fanaticism* means excessive zeal or extreme adherence to a cause.

#10: The question was:

10. Select the sentence in the passage that suggests that Jack Hill is unable to remember some specifics about his career.

The correct answer is:
The final sentence in the passage should be selected, it reads: "Plaintiff could not recall any specific location where he installed

wells and could not recall the names of any of his co-workers, other than his sister, plaintiff Jill Hill."

#11: The question was:

> For this question, consider each answer choice separately and choose all correct answer choices.

11. Which of these statements can be inferred from the passage?

|A| Jack and Jill installed some wells and fountains inside of buildings.

|B| Jack and Jill worked together more often once they went into business together.

|C| Jill was probably also exposed to asbestos.

The correct answers are:
|B| Jack and Jill worked together more often once they went into business together.

|C| Jill was probably also exposed to asbestos.

This is why:
Note that the instructions tell you to consider each answer choice separately and **choose all correct answer choices**.
- **Choice B** is correct because the passage states that from 1952 to 1958 Jack and Jill only occasionally worked together and then later worked together full time from 1958 to 1962, while operating a company they named after themselves. It reads, "Plaintiff occasionally installed wells with his sister

between approximately 1952 and 1958 ("every once in a blue moon"). T1:2-3:4. Between 1958 and 1962, Plaintiff worked full-time with his sister installing wells. T1:2-3:4. They operated a well installation company named Jack & Jill Wells."

- **Choice C** is correct because the passage says Jack was exposed while working with Jill installing wells. So we can infer that Jill worked around the same materials with similar exposure as Jack. The passage states, "Plaintiff testified that he was exposed to asbestos contained in wells while he worked as a well installer with his sister."
- **Choice A** is incorrect because the passage states the wells they installed were "installed wells outside of residential homes and commercial buildings" to the extent Jack can recall.

#12: The question was:

For this question, consider each answer choice separately and choose all correct answer choices.

12. Which of the following is needed by Plaintiffs Jack and Jill Hill to strengthen their claim or argument and win this lawsuit in court?

|A| A delineated argument explaining how the exposure to asbestos caused them harm.

|B| Specific opponents who caused the harm, whom Jack and Jill will sue for money.

|C| Nothing, Jack and Jill are ready.

The correct answers are:

[A]   A delineated argument explaining how the exposure to asbestos caused them harm.

[B]   Specific opponents who caused the harm, whom Jack and Jill will sue for money.

This is why:
Note that the instructions tell you to consider each answer choice separately, and **choose all correct answer choices**.
- **Choice A** is correct because the passage provides a great deal of factual information, but does not make an argument.
- **Choice B** is correct because the passage does not say who is to be blamed for the problem. To be strong, Jack and Jill's claim or argument should say whose conduct they are against. An argument should take issue with someone (or something); as it is, it is not directed against anyone.
- **Choice C** is incorrect because the factual information does not provide an argument or a claim that is complete.

RESEARCH **PREP.** GRE

www.research-prep.com

Research**Prep.**GRE

Reading Comprehension Passage #4

Question Set

Graduation from high school is a prerequisite to entering college. A prerequisite is a requirement that a student must complete before taking the next step. It is usually used in the context of coursework. For example, a student must complete the course "German Language One" with a passing grade before he may take "German Language Two." Every student should consider how to best structure his high school coursework in a way that ensures that he graduates on time and in a way that positions him in the best possible way to be admitted to college when he applies near the end of his high school years.

13. The author's tone can best be described as –
(A) animated.
(B) colloquial.
(C) bellicose.
(D) dissonant.
(E) explanatory.

14. The author of this passage is primarily concerned with –
(A) encouraging students to study German.
(B) explaining the word prerequisite.

(C) structuring high school coursework properly.

(D) positioning a student for successful college admissions and a timely high school graduation, by instructing the student to follow certain steps.

(E) encouraging students to apply to college after studying hard in high school.

> For this question, consider each answer choice separately and choose all correct answer choices.

15. Which of these phrases would clarify the word "positions" in the context of the passage?

A	"Keeps his options open."
B	"Creates an opening."
C	"Puts the student in the best place possible for…"

ResearchPrep.GRE

Reading Comprehension Passage #4
Answers and Explanations

The passage was:

Graduation from high school is a prerequisite to entering college. A prerequisite is a requirement that a student must complete before taking the next step. It is usually used in the context of coursework. For example, a student must complete the course "German Language One" with a passing grade before he may take "German Language Two." Every student should consider how to best structure his high school coursework in a way that ensures that he graduates on time and in a way that positions him in the best possible way to be admitted to college when he applies near the end of his high school years.

#13: The question was:

13. The author's tone can best be described as –
- (A) animated.
- (B) colloquial.
- (C) bellicose.
- (D) dissonant.
- (E) explanatory.

The correct answer is:
(E) explanatory.

This is why:
- **Choice E** is correct because *explanatory* means to explain or inform, it also means expository. Of the answer choices, this must be the correct answer based on the meanings of each potential choice.
- **Choice A** is incorrect because *animated* means spirited or lively.
- **Choice B** is incorrect because *colloquial* means using common speech, or conversational.
- **Choice C** is incorrect because *bellicose* means argumentative, warlike, or seeking a fight.
- **Choice D** is incorrect because *dissonant* means discordant, or not harmonious.

#14: The question was:

14. The author of this passage is primarily concerned with –

(A) encouraging students to study German.

(B) explaining the word prerequisite.

(C) structuring high school coursework properly.

(D) positioning a student for successful college admissions and a timely high school graduation, by instructing the student to follow certain steps.

(E) encouraging students to apply to college after studying hard in high school.

RESEARCH **PREP.** GRE

www.research-prep.com

The correct answer is:
(D) positioning a student for successful college admissions and a timely high school graduation, by instructing the student to follow certain steps.

This is why:
- **Choice D** is correct because the last sentence of the passage shows us that the goal of the passage is to position the student for successful college admissions. That sentence also mentions the goal of graduating from high school on time. Earlier in the passage the author instructs the student to follow course scheduling steps to meet the goal.
- **Choice A, B, C, and E** are incorrect because although the passage discusses (or mentions) these topics, they are not the primary purpose of the passage. The author's primary concern encompasses more than each of these parts.

#15: The question was:

For this question, consider each answer choice separately and choose all correct answer choices.

15. Which of these phrases would clarify the word "positions" in the context of the passage?

A	"Keeps his options open."
B	"Creates an opening."
C	"Puts the student in the best place possible for…"

The Verbal Reasoning and Analytical Writing Measures

The correct answer is:

C   "Puts the student in the best place possible for…"

This is why:
Here, while multiple answers may be selected, the only correct answer is answer choice C, "puts the student in the best place possible for…" successful college admissions. While he is keeping his options open by doing well, "positions" denotes a certain spot or posture, it goes beyond open options.

> ResearchPrep.GRE
>
> Reading Comprehension Passage #5
> Question Set

    A person might have an overarching belief, which can be phrased as "I should not lie because it is wrong, and I will get caught lying, which will be embarrassing and upsetting." However, even with an overarching belief not to lie, the person may have underlying sub-beliefs. For example, he might phrase this as "I want this particular conversation to be quick and easy and to go my way, and most likely I will not convince you with the truth, so I give up and lie instead."

    The overarching belief (not to lie) and the sub-belief (to lie in a particular conversation to be convincing) are hierarchical. The overarching belief (not to lie) is a more important belief to the person, and the sub-belief (to lie in the particular conversation) is a lesser belief that he sometimes slips into, or falls back on, when he is too weak to maintain his overarching belief (not to lie).

16. The passage implies that people sometimes –

(A) act irrationally.

(B) lie due to weakness even when they believe it is important, overall, to tell the truth.

(C) tell the truth because they no longer have the strength or energy to lie.

(D) believe that giving up is not wrong in some situations.

E) feel stronger when they tell the truth.

17. The author of the passage appears to believe that people –

A) try to do the right thing, but are sometimes unable to do it.

B) lie more often than they tell the truth.

C) have difficulty convincing others that they are right.

D) argue too often and try to avoid arguments by lying.

E) sometimes lie despite believing that as a general rule, people should tell the truth.

> For this question, consider each answer choice separately and choose all correct answer choices.

18. Which of these words and phrases would clarify the word "hierarchical" in the context of the passage?

A "Organized according to a structure of superiority and inferiority."

B "Each arranged according to its importance, with the ones having more importance being given priority."

C "Prioritized"

19. The main point of the passage is best described as –

A) delineating how to avoid arguments by lying.

B) reconciling a person's belief that people should not lie with his conduct of lying, by describing the concept of a sub-belief and explaining how the two types of beliefs can coexist.

(C) describing ways we communicate with others including lying to them, while not being fully morally reprehensible.

(D) discussing important beliefs and less important beliefs.

(E) describing the morally superior act of telling the truth, and the morally inferior act of lying.

ResearchPrep.GRE

Reading Comprehension Passage #5
Answers and Explanations

The passage was:

A person might have an overarching belief, which can be phrased as "I should not lie because it is wrong, and I will get caught lying, which will be embarrassing and upsetting." However, even with an overarching belief not to lie, the person may have underlying sub-beliefs. For example, he might phrase this as "I want this particular conversation to be quick and easy and to go my way, and most likely I will not convince you with the truth, so I give up and lie instead."

The overarching belief (not to lie) and the sub-belief (to lie in a particular conversation to be convincing) are hierarchical. The overarching belief (not to lie) is a more important belief to the person, and the sub-belief (to lie in the particular conversation) is a lesser belief that he sometimes slips into, or falls back on, when he is too weak to maintain his overarching belief (not to lie).

#16: The question was:

16. The passage implies that people sometimes –

(A) act irrationally.

(B) lie due to weakness even when they believe it is important, overall, to tell the truth.

(C) tell the truth because they no longer have the strength or energy to lie.

(D) believe that giving up is not wrong in some situations.

(E) feel stronger when they tell the truth.

The correct answer is:
(B) lie due to weakness even when they believe it is important, overall, to tell the truth.

This is why:
- **Choice B** is correct because the passage discusses a person falling short of their more important belief (not to lie) because he is too weak, and he wants to be convincing in a particular conversation, so he lies.
- **Choice A** is incorrect because the passage does not discuss irrational actions, and if an argument can be made for them, that inference is still somewhat removed from the text. This means that it would take several logical steps to argue for this as a textual inference. Therefore, it is not as good as choice B.
- **Choice C** is incorrect because it presents a divergent perspective from the discussion in the passage.
- **Choice D** is incorrect because giving up and lying is easier (and more convenient) according to the passage, but the passage does not say whether the author believes it is "right" or "wrong" to give up. However, the passage does say the overarching belief is that lying is wrong.
- **Choice E** is incorrect because the passage does not address whether people gain strength from telling the truth.

#17: The question was:

17. The author of the passage appears to believe that people –

(A) try to do the right thing, but are sometimes unable to do it.

(B) lie more often than they tell the truth.

(C) have difficulty convincing others that they are right.

(D) argue too often and try to avoid arguments by lying.

(E) sometimes lie despite believing that as a general rule, people should tell the truth.

The correct answer is:
(E) sometimes lie despite believing that as a general rule, people should tell the truth.

This is why:
The "best of the best" and the "best of the bad."
Remember that on the GRE, sometimes two or more answer choices work well. You must choose the better of the two good choices. Research Prep. calls this the "best of the best" dilemma. Remember, you may have two or more great choices, try to pick the best one. This also works the other way, you may have all bad answer choices. Not one is good enough to be the answer to the question. Research Prep. calls this the problem of the "best of the bad." When all of the answer choices are bad ones, pick the best of the bad choices.

Here **Choice A** is incorrect because it is not as good of an answer choice as **Choice E**. E is better than A because E contains a more detailed and fully stated accurate response. Notably, E is also better than C, another potentially correct answer choice.

- **Choice B** is incorrect because how often people lie is not discussed in the passage.
- **Choice C** is incorrect because the passage does not address this as fully as answer choice E.
- **Choice D** is incorrect because the passage does not discuss arguing directly, and there are several better answer choices.

RESEARCH **PREP.** GRE
www.research-prep.com

#18: The question was:

> For this question, consider each answer choice separately and choose all correct answer choices.

18. Which of these words and phrases would clarify the word "hierarchical" in the context of the passage?

|A| "Organized according to a structure of superiority and inferiority."

|B| "Each arranged according to its importance, with the ones having more importance being given priority."

|C| "Prioritized"

The correct answers are:
All three answers are correct.

|A| "Organized according to a structure of superiority and inferiority."

|B| "Each arranged according to its importance, with the ones having more importance being given priority."

|C| "Prioritized"

This is why:
The correct answers are A, B, and C because all three of these answers would clarify the word "hierarchical" as used within the context of the passage. They all depict the meaning of that term in a way that would add clarity to the text.

RESEARCH **PREP.** GRE
www.research-prep.com

#19: The question was:

19. The main point of the passage is best described as –

(A) delineating how to avoid arguments by lying.

(B) reconciling a person's belief that people should not lie with his conduct of lying, by describing the concept of a sub-belief and explaining how the two types of beliefs can coexist.

(C) describing ways we communicate with others including lying to them, while not being fully morally reprehensible.

(D) discussing important beliefs and less important beliefs.

(E) describing the morally superior act of telling the truth, and the morally inferior act of lying.

The correct answer is:
(B) reconciling a person's belief that people should not lie with his conduct of lying, by describing the concept of a sub-belief and explaining how the two types of beliefs can coexist.

This is why:
- **Choice B** is correct because the passage explains how people believe they should not lie (their overarching belief) and then reconcile their conduct when they lie by describing a sub-belief and explaining it.
- **Choice A** is incorrect because the main concern of the passage is not avoiding arguments.
- **Choice C** is incorrect because the person lying does so for a practical reason and because he is too weak to maintain his

ideal. The passage does not say lying is not fully morally reprehensible; it only says it is practical.
- **Choice D** is incorrect because it is not as good of an answer as choice B. B is better because it is more descriptive and is also accurate.
- **Choice E** is incorrect because it is not as good of an answer choice as B.

ResearchPrep.GRE

Reading Comprehension Passage #6
Question Set

A sailor's knowledge of knot tying can include knots such as the "Manharness Knot" the "Carrick Bend" and the "Surgeon's Knot." Knowledge of knot tying can provide a sailor (or fisherman) with options for handling different tasks, which require stronger holds, thicker or thinner ropes, or the ability to quickly loosen or untie a rope. However, in modern day sailing, knowing how to tie a "Good Luck Knot" seems irrelevant to many recreational boaters.

20. Select the sentence in which the author implies that despite their usefulness, learning to tie knots is an antiquated practice.

21. If it is true that knowledge of knot tying provides sailors with options for handling different tasks, then which of these answer choices most plausibly shows why knot tying may at the same time be irrelevant to recreational sailors?

A) Knot tying is specifically helpful to certain kinds of sails, especially those found on small boats.

B) Even when a sailor has mastered knot tying, he may at times become confused and tie the wrong knot, which is not helpful in many situations.

(C) It is time-consuming to learn to tie knots.

(D) Learning to tie various types of knots is time-consuming, and knots are unnecessary with today's sailing technology.

(E) Learning to tie various types of knots is time-consuming, and it is more important to spend time mastering other aspects of sailing.

22. Which statement explains why a recreational sailor would learn to tie various knots, even though other sailors believe them to be unnecessary?

(A) The sailor is not concerned with the opinions of other sailors.

(B) The sailor is new to sailing.

(C) The sailor finds knot tying to be restful because it reminds him of long ago, and he sails for relaxation.

(D) The sailor hopes to have a faster boat in comparison to other sailboats.

(E) The sailor has a variety of sails which he interchanges on his sailboat.

RESEARCH **PREP.** GRE

www.research-prep.com

Research**Prep.**GRE

Reading Comprehension Passage #6
Answers and Explanations

The passage was:

A sailor's knowledge of knot tying can include knots such as the "Manharness Knot" the "Carrick Bend" and the "Surgeon's Knot." Knowledge of knot tying can provide a sailor (or fisherman) with options for handling different tasks, which require stronger holds, thicker or thinner ropes, or the ability to quickly loosen or untie a rope. <u>However, in modern day sailing, knowing how to tie a "Good Luck Knot" seems irrelevant to many recreational boaters.</u>

#20: The question was:

20. Select the sentence in which the author implies that despite their usefulness, learning to tie knots is an antiquated practice.

The correct answer is:
"However, in modern day sailing, knowing how to tie a "Good Luck Knot" seems irrelevant to many recreational boaters."

This is why:
This sentence specifically states that "in modern day sailing" many boaters think tying a specific type of knot is irrelevant. However, it

The Verbal Reasoning and Analytical Writing Measures

implies a broader stance that all types of knots are seen as irrelevant to many modern boaters.

#21: The question was:

21. If it is true that knowledge of knot tying provides sailors with options for handling different tasks, then which of these answer choices most plausibly shows why knot tying may at the same time be irrelevant to recreational sailors?

(A) Knot tying is specifically helpful to certain kinds of sails, especially those found on small boats.

(B) Even when a sailor has mastered knot tying, he may at times become confused and tie the wrong knot, which is not helpful in many situations.

(C) It is time-consuming to learn to tie knots.

(D) Learning to tie various types of knots is time-consuming, and knots are unnecessary with today's sailing technology.

(E) Learning to tie various types of knots is time-consuming, and it is more important to spend time mastering other aspects of sailing.

The correct answer is:
(D) Learning to tie various types of knots is time-consuming, and knots are unnecessary with today's sailing technology.

This is why:
- **Choice D** is correct because it states that knot tying is time-consuming (a problem like choices B and C) and also easily replaceable with today's sailing technology. Because tying

knots is easily replaceable with technology, knot tying can be irrelevant to many recreational boaters.
- **Choice A** is incorrect because recreational sailors (boaters) would often sail small boats.
- **Choice B** is incorrect because accidentally incorrectly tying the knot makes knot tying problematic, but not irrelevant.
- **Choice C** is incorrect because the difficulty of learning knot tying does not make it irrelevant.
- **Choice E** is incorrect because it does not show how knot tying is irrelevant. It just states that other tasks should be mastered first. Knot tying is a relevant task but not one of the most relevant tasks.

#22: The question was:

22. Which statement explains why a recreational sailor would learn to tie various knots, even though other sailors believe them to be unnecessary?

(A) The sailor is not concerned with the opinions of other sailors.

(B) The sailor is new to sailing.

(C) The sailor finds knot tying to be restful because it reminds him of long ago, and he sails for relaxation.

(D) The sailor hopes to have a faster boat in comparison to other sailboats.

(E) The sailor has a variety of sails which he interchanges on his sailboat.

The correct answer is:
(C) The sailor finds knot tying to be restful because it reminds him of long ago, and he sails for relaxation.

This is why:
- **Choice C** is correct because we have an actual reason for tying knots. This sailor finds knot tying to be restful. He also sails to relax. Therefore, learning to tie knots would be good for him (increasing his goal of relaxation) while irrelevant to other boaters (who sail for other reasons, like fun or speed, or find knot tying agitating).
- **Choice A** is incorrect because it says he is not swayed by others' opinions. But, even when we know he is making his own choice (free of others' influence), we still do not know why he chooses to tie knots. So, the substance of the question (why would he learn to tie knots?) remains unanswered.
- **Choice B** is incorrect. At first glance, a test-taker might think the new sailor is mistakenly tying knots and will stop later when he learns of the available alternatives that make knot tying irrelevant. However, this analysis relies on information not present in the answer choice. Beware of adding information to the answer choice in this way. The actual answer choice B gives us very little information. Even though this sailor is new, he might not be mistaken. So, we still do not know the reason he would learn to tie various knots.
- **Choice D** is incorrect because the passage does not say knot tying makes boats faster.
- **Choice E** is incorrect because other modern day boaters may also interchange sails and still find knot tying irrelevant. So, it is not as good as choice C.

RESEARCH **PREP.** GRE

www.research-prep.com

> Research**Prep**.GRE
>
> Reading Comprehension Passage #7
>
> Question Set

Scientist Pierre Duhem wrote that an experiment consists of empirical evidence and the scientist's interpretation of that evidence through his knowledgeable expertise. Duhem recognized that the scientist interprets the observable evidence during his work and then forms theories. Duhem stated that experiments require both the observation of data and the scientist's interpretation of that data.

23. Which of these would weaken the passage the most, if true?

(A) Scientists do not use knowledge to interpret data.

(B) Experiments are more complex then presented.

(C) Experiments involve hypotheses.

(D) Non-scientists also interpret data.

(E) Theories are often inaccurate.

For this question, consider each answer choice separately and choose all correct answer choices.

24. Which of these events demonstrates Duhem's belief as presented in the passage?

|225|

The Verbal Reasoning and Analytical Writing Measures

| A | A scientist reviews population growth and food consumption in various nations and compares this information. She concludes that populations expand more quickly in areas with larger amounts of food consumption.

| B | A scientist researches articles stating stars contain certain natural elements. She writes a paper reviewing the articles she has read, explaining that the articles would be useful instruction materials in high school classrooms.

| C | A scientist considers the growth of a tree that has been exposed to polluted water and develops the belief that trees are less likely to grow quickly in a polluted environment.

25. Which word most closely matches the meaning of the word "interpretation" used in the context of the final sentence of the passage?

(A) Analogy
(B) Recognition
(C) Contention
(D) Distinguish
(E) Analysis

RESEARCH **PREP.** GRE

www.research-prep.com

Research**Prep.**GRE

Reading Comprehension Passage #7

Answers and Explanations

The passage was:

Scientist Pierre Duhem wrote that an experiment consists of empirical evidence and the scientist's interpretation of that evidence through his knowledgeable expertise. Duhem recognized that the scientist interprets the observable evidence during his work and then forms theories. Duhem stated that experiments require both the observation of data and the scientist's interpretation of that data.

#23: The question was:

23. Which of these would weaken the passage the most, if true?

(A) Scientists do not use knowledge to interpret data.

(B) Experiments are more complex then presented.

(C) Experiments involve hypotheses.

(D) Non-scientists also interpret data.

(E) Theories are often inaccurate.

The Verbal Reasoning and Analytical Writing Measures

The correct answer is:
(A) Scientists do not use knowledge to interpret data.

This is why:
- **Choice A** is correct because the crux of the passage's argument is (1) scientists have data; (2) they interpret it; and (3) they form an idea (theory) explaining it. Without knowledgably interpreting the data the scientist cannot transition from data to theory and the passage is weakened.
- **Choice B** is incorrect because even if this analysis if simplified, if the simple analysis can accurately apply to a complex experiment, it is not weakened.
- **Choice C** is incorrect because it is not necessarily contradictory to the simple analysis. If the simple analysis works for a complex experiment, it can work for C as well.
- **Choice D** is incorrect because the passage does not exclude non-scientists also interpreting data. It does not appear to be exclusive; the passage just does not address non-scientists.
- **Choice E** is incorrect because the accuracy of the theory (whether the theory is correct or incorrect) is not addressed in the passage, and it is not weaker if this additional information were to be added and discussed.

#24: The question was:

For this question, consider each answer choice separately and choose all correct answer choices.

24. Which of these events demonstrates Duhem's belief as presented in the passage?

|A| A scientist reviews population growth and food consumption in various nations and compares this information. She concludes that populations expand more quickly in areas with larger amounts of food consumption.

|B| A scientist researches articles stating stars contain certain natural elements. She writes a paper reviewing the articles she has read, explaining that the articles would be useful instruction materials in high school classrooms.

|C| A scientist considers the growth of a tree that has been exposed to polluted water and develops the belief that trees are less likely to grow quickly in a polluted environment.

The correct answers are:

|A| A scientist reviews population growth and food consumption in various nations and compares this information. She concludes that populations expand more quickly in areas with larger amounts of food consumption.

|C| A scientist considers the growth of a tree that has been exposed to polluted water and develops the belief that trees are less likely to grow quickly in a polluted environment.

This is why:
- **Choice A** is correct because it involves (1) data (information on population growth and food consumption); (2) the interpretation of that data (the scientist's comparing and consideration of the data to hopefully reach a conclusion); and (3) formation of a theory (the scientist's conclusion that populations expand more quickly in areas with greater food consumption).

- **Choice C** is correct because the scientist's work involves (1) data (tree growth and polluted water); (2) the interpretation of the data (considering the effect of polluted water on the growth of trees); and (3) the formation of a theory (the scientist forms the belief that trees are less likely to grow quickly in a polluted environment).
- **Choice B** is incorrect because the scientist does not form a theory about the data (regarding the composition of the stars). She just decides that the articles are useful teaching materials for high school classrooms.

#25: The question was:

25. Which word most closely matches the meaning of the word "interpretation" used in the context of the final sentence of the passage?

(A) Analogy
(B) Recognition
(C) Contention
(D) Distinguish
(E) Analysis

The correct answer is:
(E) Analysis

This is why:
- **Choice E** is correct because *analysis* means to consider using reason or to understand or explain. Choice E is more similar to interpretation as used in the context of the final sentence of the passage then the other answer choices.
- **Choice A** is incorrect because *analogy* means similarity, or parallel comparison.
- **Choice B** is incorrect because *recognition* means to see something for what it is, or to acknowledge something.
- **Choice C** is incorrect because *contention* means a claim, or an argument.
- **Choice D** is incorrect because *distinguish* means to discern that one thing is different from another.

ResearchPrep.GRE

Reading Comprehension Passage #8
Question Set

An American white pelican (*pelecanuserythrorhynychos*) has a nine-foot wingspan. While it is called a white pelican, it can be easily distinguished from a swan because a swan has no black in its wings, while a white pelican's wings are partly black. A snow goose is distinguishable by its comparatively small size. But Gannets, which can be found along the Florida coastline, are sometimes mistaken for white pelicans.

> For this question, consider each answer choice separately and choose all correct answer choices.

26. The author of this passage would probably agree that –

A. These birds can, at times, be found in areas nearby one another, making it important to show bird watchers how to distinguish them from each other.

B. Bird watchers seek to distinguish birds based on the appearance of the bird.

C. Bird watching is a lost pastime, which vanished long ago because of its tiresome nature.

27. Which word would accurately replace "comparatively" as used in this context?

(A) Uniquely
(B) Divergently
(C) Relatively
(D) Own
(E) Displayed

RESEARCH **PREP.** GRE

www.research-prep.com

Research**Prep.**GRE

Reading Comprehension Passage #8
Answers and Explanations

The passage was:

An American white pelican (*pelecanuserythrorhynychos*) has a nine-foot wingspan. While it is called a white pelican, it can be easily distinguished from a swan because a swan has no black in its wings, while a white pelican's wings are partly black. A snow goose is distinguishable by its comparatively small size. But Gannets, which can be found along the Florida coastline, are sometimes mistaken for white pelicans.

#26: **The question was:**

For this question, consider each answer choice separately and choose all correct answer choices.

26. The author of this passage would probably agree that -

A   These birds can, at times, be found in areas nearby one another, making it important to show bird watchers how to distinguish them from each other.

B   Bird watchers seek to distinguish birds based on the appearance of the bird.

|234|

The Verbal Reasoning and Analytical Writing Measures

RESEARCH PREP. GRE

www.research-prep.com

|C| Bird watching is a lost pastime, which vanished long ago because of its tiresome nature.

The correct answers are:

|A| These birds can, at times, be found in areas nearby one another, making it important to show bird watchers how to distinguish them from each other.

|B| Bird watchers seek to distinguish birds based on the appearance of the bird.

This is why:

Test-taker tip: none of these answer choices remain neutral regarding how to interpret the passage. Because of the answer choices (rather than the passage), you must decide if the best answer choices require the passage to be written for bird watchers or if bird watching no longer exists.

- **Choice A** is correct because the passage seeks to show readers how to distinguish these birds from one another. Therefore, it seems that the author thinks people looking at birds will need help telling them apart, and this is necessary if the birds' locations overlap at times.
- **Choice B** is correct because the passage seeks to tell readers how to distinguish these birds from one another based on their appearance when they see them.
- **Choice C** is incorrect because the passage is more likely to be geared toward readers who are bird watchers (choices A and B) rather than saying bird watching has vanished (choice C).

#27: The question was:

27. Which word would accurately replace "comparatively" as used in this context?

(A) Uniquely
(B) Divergently
(C) Relatively
(D) Own
(E) Displayed

The correct answer is:
(C) Relatively

This is why:
Test-taker tip: The correct answer to this question should maintain the author's meaning in the original passage to the closest extent possible. Even though other answer choices can work, they are incorrect if they do not provide the same, or nearly the same meaning as the word "comparatively" in the original passage.

- **Choice C** is correct because *relatively* is a close synonym for comparatively, and since they mean the same thing in the context, this is the best answer choice.
- **Choice A** is incorrect because *uniquely* means individually, or distinctively, which is not as similar to comparatively as relatively (choice C).
- **Choice B** is incorrect because *divergently* means to deviate from, or move away from, which is also not as similar to comparatively as relatively (choice C).

- **Choice D** is incorrect because *own* means personal or specific.
- **Choice E** is incorrect because *displayed* means exhibited or shown.

RESEARCH **PREP.** GRE

www.research-prep.com

> Research**Prep**.GRE
>
> Reading Comprehension Passage #9
> # Question Set

   Every human being has moral dignity. Moral dignity is intrinsic moral value or intrinsic moral worth, which a person has by virtue of being human. A victim's moral dignity is not destroyed or reduced by being the victim of an offense. When an offender has harmed a victim, the victim is certainly still a person of worth.

28. Select the sentence in the passage which explains why the author believes a person has moral dignity.

29. The author discusses "moral dignity" primarily to –
(A) describe what it is and its value.
(B) acknowledge the harm victims can suffer at the hands of criminals.
(C) explore human conduct and response.
(D) argue that victims of crime are valuable and have worth no matter what another has done to them.
(E) argue that crime does no real harm to victims, because all people recover from an offense.

30. Based on the passage we can conclude that –

(A) a person can destroy his own value, but another cannot do it to him.

(B) every person has intrinsic moral value regardless of what another may do.

(C) no person can degrade himself by his own conduct.

(D) some people act with dignity and some do not, but ultimately they are basically the same.

(E) we are all equal, regardless of how we may act.

ResearchPrep.GRE

Reading Comprehension Passage #9
Answers and Explanations

The passage was:

Every human being has moral dignity. <u>Moral dignity is intrinsic moral value or intrinsic moral worth, which a person has by virtue of being human.</u> A victim's moral dignity is not destroyed or reduced by being the victim of an offense. When an offender has harmed a victim, the victim is certainly still a person of worth.

#28: The question was:

28. Select the sentence in the passage which explains why the author believes a person has moral dignity.

The correct answer is:

"Moral dignity is intrinsic moral value or intrinsic moral worth, which a person has by virtue of being human."

This is why:

This is the correct answer because "by virtue of" in this context most nearly means "because." So, a person has moral dignity "by virtue of" or "because" he is human. This sentence is a better choice than the first sentence because the first sentence states the claim, but does not provide any insight into why. The correct answer (the second sentence) shows us that the author believes every human has moral dignity because they are human.

#29: The question was:

29. The author discusses "moral dignity" primarily to –
- (A) describe what it is and its value.
- (B) acknowledge the harm victims can suffer at the hands of criminals.
- (C) explore human conduct and response.
- (D) argue that victims of crime are valuable and have worth no matter what another has done to them.
- (E) argue that crime does no real harm to victims, because all people recover from an offense.

The correct answer is:
(D) argue that victims of crime are valuable and have worth no matter what another has done to them.

This is why:
- **Choice D** is correct because it accurately relates to the text of the passage, and gives a more thorough description of the text. Choice D sums up the primary aim of the author better than the other choices.
- **Choices A, B and C**, are incorrect, primarily because they are not as good as answer choice D.
- **Choice E** is incorrect because it is not an accurate description of the text. The text only discusses moral dignity

(intrinsic moral value or worth), not harm to a victim's body (such as an injury) or property (like loss from theft). So, the passage does not state crime does not harm victims (which is choice E's interpretation).

#30: The question was:

30. Based on the passage we can conclude that –
   (A) a person can destroy his own value, but another cannot do it to him.
   (B) every person has intrinsic moral value regardless of what another may do.
   (C) no person can degrade himself by his own conduct.
   (D) some people act with dignity and some do not, but ultimately they are basically the same.
   (E) we are all equal, regardless of how we may act.

The correct answer is:
(B) every person has intrinsic moral value regardless of what another may do.

This is why:
- **Choice B** is correct because it is an accurate re-statement of the argument made in the passage.
- **Choices A, C, D and E** are incorrect because they are not supported by the passage.

CHAPTER #4

THE VERBAL REASONING MEASURE

Timed Question Practice Sets

RESEARCH **PREP.** GRE

www.research-prep.com

Timed Practice Question Set #1

Time – 30 Minutes

> GRE Instructions: Select the <u>two</u> answer choices that, when used to complete the sentence, fit the meaning of the sentence as a whole <u>and</u> produce completed sentences that are alike in meaning.

1. We are almost all universally _____ to present ourselves well in social situations, so as to gain the favor of others.

A	transformed
B	ingenuous
C	illuminating
D	prone
E	unlikely
F	apt

2. The rough jokes of the two teenage boys startled the young mother by their _____.

| A | deviousness |
| B | discretion |

|245|

The Verbal Reasoning and Analytical Writing Measures

C	fluency
D	garrulous nature
E	imprudence
F	impudence

> GRE Instructions: For each blank select one entry from the corresponding column of choices. Fill all blanks in the way that best completes the text.

3. The _____ performance was excellent. Despite it being "off the cuff," it was interesting and funny.

- A) improvident
- B) contentious
- C) impromptu
- D) acerbic
- E) refined

4. While hanging out with his friends, he was quick-witted and free with (i)_____ and sarcasm. But around women, he was accidentally (ii)_____, rebuffing them unnecessarily.

Blank (i)	Blank (ii)
A) quips	D) whimsical

B	questions	E	recalcitrant
C	travail	F	profound

Reading Comprehension Passage

Evelyn Fox Keller argues that scientists can accidentally incorporate gender bias into their work despite a scientist's own belief that he is not biased. Keller seeks to help scientists to see the accidental interjection of bias into their projects to help scientists address the problem. Accidental incorporation of bias interjects the scientist's own beliefs (subjectivity) into a scientific project in a way that undermines the empirical (objective) accuracy of the project.

Choose one correct answer choice for each question.

5. From the highlighted sentence, we can infer that —

A) scientists do not try to separate their personal beliefs from their scientific conclusions.

B) scientists' biases, rather than their mistakes, undermine accuracy.

C) scientists' biases sometimes harm scientific results accidentally by compromising accuracy.

D) a scientist's beliefs are harmful to scientific projects.

E) scientists undermine their own results.

6. Based on the passage as a whole, we can infer that –

(A) there is no way to curtail scientists' incorporation of gender bias into their projects.

(B) scientists generally agree with Keller's conclusions about the incorporation of bias.

(C) scientists generally agree that gender bias exists.

(D) scientists know when they incorporate bias into a project.

(E) Keller is attempting to make scientific projects more accurate by showing scientists a hidden problem.

For this question, consider each answer choice separately and choose all correct answer choices.

7. Based on the passage, scientists might respond to Keller by –

[A]   stating that Keller has shown them a hidden problem that they can now address.

[B]   stating that they are not biased.

[C]   stating that Keller is incorrect.

Reading Comprehension Passage

Reverend Martin Luther King Jr.'s teachings of forgiveness promoted an understanding of personal value that is separate from the way one is treated by others. A harmful person does not determine your worth, or your response, instead, you do. Reverend

King requested that we respond to hate with love and know that our provision of love increases our own worth. This was an effective, significant way to promote positivity in the midst of harm and knowledge that each person chooses his own response to the conduct of another. Reverend King promoted a version of forgiveness where the forgiver heightens her own value by forgiving someone who does not deserve it. The forgiver becomes the "better person" by loving her aggressor.

> For this question, consider each answer choice separately and choose all correct answer choices.

8. Which of these statements does the passage support?

A   A person becomes a "better person" by loving another regardless of his conduct.

B   When one harms another, the person harmed should "right the wrong" by requesting the harmful person apologize and make amends.

C   A person becomes a "better person" by holding another accountable.

9. Select the sentence which best states the author's claim that "you increase your self-worth."

Choose one correct answer choice for each question.

10. Which of these explains the relationship of the first sentence to the rest of the passage?

(A) It compares one position to another and goes on to explain the comparison in the rest of the passage.

(B) It explains the view which is further examined in the rest of the passage.

(C) It provides a generalization which is examined in detail in the remainder of the passage.

(D) It provides a view and the rest of the passage provides an antithesis to it.

(E) It asks a question that is answered by the rest of the passage.

11. In this context, "provision" most nearly means –

(A) zealous.
(B) corpus.
(C) exchange.
(D) gift.
(E) mature.

GRE Instructions: Select the two answer choices that, when used to complete the sentence, fit the meaning of the sentence as a whole and produce completed sentences that are alike in meaning.

12. The tenacious owl kept his perch, despite the _____ fire.

A	flourishing
B	monotonous
C	noxious
D	commencing
E	sweeping
F	obvious

13. Social distinctions or _____ are bad for societies that wish to foster democratic communities.

A	epidemics
B	hierarchies
C	demographics
D	classes
E	clamor
F	fundamentals

RESEARCH **PREP.** GRE
www.research-prep.com

> GRE Instructions: For each blank select one entry from the corresponding column of choices. Fill all blanks in the way that best completes the text.

14. The political candidate stated to the audience, that his speech would be (i)_____; it would only address a limited portion of the topic. He did this to (ii)_____ a previous statement in which he made a mistake, but still (iii)_____ his political opponent.

Blank (i)	Blank (ii)	Blank (iii)
A) qualified	D) ponder	G) recast
B) prominent	E) recant	H) refute
C) motley	F) muse over	I) quandary

15. The nun's _____ could not be mistaken; she was a true example of faithfulness and goodness.

A) fawning
B) piety
C) hyperbole
D) mnemonic
E) platitude

16. Mountain climbing involves not only (i) _____ to work hard and a lack of (ii)_____ from an exercise plan, but also understanding how to deal with the elements and prevent harm to oneself from (iii)_____ while climbing mountains in difficult or changing conditions.

Blank (i)	Blank (ii)	Blank (iii)
(A) taut	(D) deviation	(G) exposure
(B) determination	(E) rancor	(H) regeneration
(C) rendering	(F) emergence	(I) symbiosis

Reading Comprehension Passage

Rodeos are sometimes considered to be venues for the display of skills which, while exciting, are useless. However, learning the skills to control livestock is still crucial in many rural parts of the United States. Proponents of rodeos believe that by raising excitement for viewing expert displays of these skills in action, more young people will learn them. They believe this, in part, because more people will want to learn how to control livestock if it is seen as exciting to be good at it.

Choose one correct answer choice for each question.

17. In this passage, the author's position is –

(A) that rodeos have proponents who believe they are necessary, but the author remains neutral.

B) rodeos are necessary in many rural places within the United States.

C) rodeos are exciting but useless.

D) rodeos are exciting and either useless or crucial, but the author does not conclude either way.

E) rodeos create reasons for young people to learn dangerous skills for entertainment.

18. Based on the passage, each of the following is a reason proponents believe young people train to participate in rodeos EXCEPT —

A) they are excited.

B) they want to become experts.

C) they have seen rodeos.

D) they want to become fit.

E) they want to learn skills.

19. Which of these best sets forth the reason for the first two sentences of the passage?

A) To explain a problem which needs a solution.

B) To explain that what is useless to one person may be crucial to another.

C) To showcase the difference between an urban view and a rural view on the same topic.

(D) To succinctly present two sides of an ongoing argument.

(E) To argue against rodeos and then change tactics and argue for them.

20. Which of these actions if performed would help solve this debate?

(A) The provision of information about the usefulness of rodeos by proponents to those who disagree.

(B) Continuing to have rodeos.

(C) Continuing to train for rodeos.

(D) Encouraging excitement for watching rodeos.

(E) Explaining the great danger of participating in a rodeo.

RESEARCH **PREP.** GRE

www.research-prep.com

> Research**Prep.**GRE
>
> Timed Practice Question Set #1
> # Answers and Explanations

#1: The question was:

1. We are almost all universally _____ to present ourselves well in social situations, so as to gain the favor of others.

- [A] transformed
- [B] ingenuous
- [C] illuminating
- [D] prone
- [E] unlikely
- [F] apt

The correct answers are:

- [D] prone; and
- [F] apt

|256|

The Verbal Reasoning and Analytical Writing Measures

RESEARCH PREP. GRE
www.research-prep.com

The sentence context shows:

We try to gain the admiration of others in social situations, and to do this we generally will seek to present ourselves well.

The answer choice vocabulary words and their synonyms are:

Answer Choice Vocabulary	Synonyms
Transformed	Change completely, alter
Ingenuous	Honest, truthful
Illuminating	Lighting up, incandescent; enlightening
Prone	Liable, likely, inclined
Unlikely	Not probable
Apt	Likely, inclined, disposed

#2: The question was:

2. The rough jokes of the two teenage boys startled the young mother by their _____.

- [A] deviousness
- [B] discretion
- [C] fluency
- [D] garrulous nature
- [E] imprudence
- [F] impudence

The correct answers are:

- [A] deviousness; and

|257|

The Verbal Reasoning and Analytical Writing Measures

| D | garrulous nature |

The sentence context shows:

The boys' jokes had a hard edge that was so negative it startled the young mother.

The answer choice vocabulary words and their synonyms are:

Answer Choice Vocabulary	Synonyms
Deviousness	Dishonesty, crookedness
Discretion	Caution, judgment, tact
Fluency	Ease of expression
Garrulous nature	Talkative, chatty
Imprudence	Carelessness, neglect
Impudence	Audacity, insolence, rudeness

#3: The question was:

3. The _____ performance was excellent. Despite it being "off the cuff," it was interesting and funny.

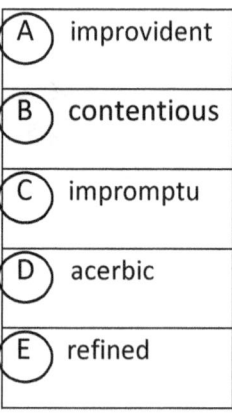

A) improvident
B) contentious
C) impromptu
D) acerbic
E) refined

RESEARCH PREP. GRE
www.research-prep.com

The correct answer is:

(C) impromptu

The answer choice vocabulary words and their synonyms are:

Answer Choice Vocabulary	Synonyms
Improvident	Extravagant spending, without thrift
Contentious	Argumentative, querulous
Impromptu	Without preparation, spur of the moment
Acerbic	Sour, bitter
Refined	Elegant, with manners, the best part of the whole

#4: The question was:

4. While hanging out with his friends, he was quick-witted and free with (i)_____ and sarcasm. But around women, he was accidentally (ii)_____, rebuffing them unnecessarily.

Blank (i)	Blank (ii)
(A) quips	(D) whimsical
(B) questions	(E) recalcitrant
(C) travail	(F) profound

The Verbal Reasoning and Analytical Writing Measures

RESEARCH PREP. GRE
www.research-prep.com

The correct answers are:

Blank (i):

(A) quips

Blank (ii):

(E) recalcitrant

The answer choice vocabulary words and their synonyms are:

Answer Choice Vocabulary	Synonyms
Quips	Witty communication, banter
Questions	Inquiries, queries
Travail	Struggle, anguish
Whimsical	Playful, fanciful
Recalcitrant	Disobedient, uncontrollable
Profound	Deep, intelligent, philosophical

Reading Comprehension Passage

The passage was:

Evelyn Fox Keller argues that scientists can accidentally incorporate gender bias into their work despite a scientist's own belief that he is not biased. Keller seeks to help scientists to see the accidental interjection of bias into their projects to help scientists address the problem. Accidental incorporation of bias interjects the scientist's own beliefs (subjectivity) into a scientific project in a way that undermines the empirical (objective) accuracy of the project.

#5: The question was:

5. From the highlighted sentence, we can infer that –

(A) scientists do not try to separate their personal beliefs from their scientific conclusions.

(B) scientists' biases, rather than their mistakes, undermine accuracy.

(C) scientists' biases sometimes harm scientific results accidentally by compromising accuracy.

(D) a scientist's beliefs are harmful to scientific projects.

(E) scientists undermine their own results.

The correct answer is:
(C) scientists' biases sometimes harm scientific results accidentally by compromising accuracy.

This is why:
- **Choice C** is correct because the highlighted sentence shows that this is true. It states "[a]ccidental incorporation of bias interjects the scientist's own beliefs" and this "undermines the empirical (objective) accuracy."
- **Choice A** is incorrect because the highlighted sentence says incorporation of personal beliefs is accidental, and there is no reason given for the scientist to undermine his own accuracy through a lack of effort.
- **Choice B** is incorrect because the incorporation of bias is the mistake addressed in the highlighted sentence. Because bias is a mistake, the answer cannot be bias *rather than* mistake.

- **Choice D** is incorrect because beliefs are only harmful if they accidentally impact the project. Other beliefs (not brought in) are not harmful. This choice is too broad, and C is a better answer choice.
- **Choice E** is incorrect because it is overly broad, and C is a better answer choice.

#6: The question was:

6. Based on the passage as a whole, we can infer that –

(A) there is no way to curtail scientists' incorporation of gender bias into their projects.

(B) scientists generally agree with Keller's conclusions about the incorporation of bias.

(C) scientists generally agree that gender bias exists.

(D) scientists know when they incorporate bias into a project.

(E) Keller is attempting to make scientific projects more accurate by showing scientists a hidden problem.

The correct answer is:
(E) Keller is attempting to make scientific projects more accurate by showing scientists a hidden problem.

This is why:
- **Choice E** is correct because the passage states Keller seeks to show scientists the problem in order to help them. Because the problem undermines accuracy, by showing

scientists the problem exists, we can infer Keller is attempting to increase accuracy.
- **Choice A** is incorrect because the passage says Keller wants "to help scientists to address the problem."
- **Choice B** is incorrect because Keller tries to help "scientists to see the accidental interjection of bias" but a "scientist's own belief that he is not biased" is also mentioned. So, we cannot infer whether scientists agree with Keller.
- **Choice C** is incorrect because we cannot infer wither scientists generally agree with Keller from the passage.
- **Choice D** is incorrect because the passage says the incorporation of bias is accidental.

#7: The question was:

For this question, consider each answer choice separately and choose all correct answer choices.

7. Based on the passage, scientists might respond to Keller by –

|A| stating that Keller has shown them a hidden problem that they can now address.

|B| stating that they are not biased.

|C| stating that Keller is incorrect.

The correct answers are:
All three answer choices!

|A| stating that Keller has shown them a hidden problem that they can now address.

|B| stating that they are not biased.

| C | stating that Keller is incorrect.

Choices A, B and C are all correct because scientists could respond to Keller's argument in any of these ways. They are all plausible based on the passage.

The passage was:

    Reverend Martin Luther King Jr.'s teachings of forgiveness promoted an understanding of personal value that is separate from the way one is treated by others. A harmful person does not determine your worth, or your response, instead, you do. Reverend King requested that we respond to hate with love and know that our provision of love increases our own worth. This was an effective, significant way to promote positivity in the midst of harm and knowledge that each person chooses his own response to the conduct of another. Reverend King promoted a version of forgiveness where the forgiver heightens her own value by forgiving someone who does not deserve it. The forgiver becomes the "better person" by loving her aggressor.

#8: The question was:

> For this question, consider each answer choice separately and choose all correct answer choices.

8. The passage supports which of these statements?

|A| A person becomes a "better person" by loving another regardless of his conduct.

|B| When one harms another, the person harmed should "right the wrong" by requesting the harmful person apologize and make amends.

|C| A person becomes a "better person" by holding another accountable.

The correct answer is:
|A| A person becomes a "better person" by loving another regardless of his conduct.

This is why:
- **Choice A** is correct because it is supported by the passage. For example, the passages states "the forgiver heightens her own value by forgiving someone who does not deserve it."
- **Choices B and C** are incorrect because neither is supported by this passage. While they are familiar, even popular ways to think, they are not present in this passage.

#9: The question was:

9. Select the sentence which best states the author's claim that "you increase your self-worth."

The correct answer is:
"A harmful person does not determine your worth or your response, instead, you do."

This is why:
- This sentence is the best choice of the possible options within the paragraph because it uses the term "worth" and directly states "you do" in relation to who determines your worth.
- It is slightly better than the second choice sentence, which reads "...our provision of love increases our own worth." This is the second choice because it is more ambiguously written and less similar to the question prompt.
- It is also better than the third best choice, which says "the forgiver heightens her own value," because "self-worth" as requested in the question prompt is closer in wording to "your worth" then "her own value."

RESEARCH **PREP.** GRE
www.research-prep.com

Test-taker tip: remember, the computer based GRE will allow you to easily underline the necessary sentence as your answer selection.

#10: The question was:

10. Which of these explains the relationship of the first sentence to the rest of the passage?

(A) It compares one position to another and goes on to explain the comparison in the rest of the passage.

(B) It explains the view which is further examined in the rest of the passage.

(C) It provides a generalization which is examined in detail in the remainder of the passage.

(D) It provides a view and the rest of the passage provides an antithesis to it.

(E) It asks a question that is answered by the rest of the passage.

The correct answer is:
(B) It explains the view which is further examined in the rest of the passage.

This is why:
- **Choice B** is correct because the first sentence sets forth an explanation of the view ("...personal value that is separate from the way one is treated by others"). Then that view is examined in the passage (how and by whom personal worth is determined).

The Verbal Reasoning and Analytical Writing Measures

- **Choice A** is incorrect because the first sentence does not compare one view to another view. It only presents a single view.
- **Choice C** is incorrect because the first sentence states that it is Reverend Martin Luther King Jr.'s teaching (his view). Nothing shows it is a generalization of a topic.
- **Choice D** is incorrect because the rest of the passage does not seek to disprove the view or show that it is wrong.
- **Choice E** is incorrect because the first sentence does not ask a question.

#11: The question was:

11. In this context, "provision" most nearly means –

(A) zealous.
(B) corpus.
(C) exchange.
(D) gift.
(E) mature.

The correct answer is:
(D) gift.

This is why:
- **Choice D** is correct because *provision* in this context most nearly means to provide love without expecting or needing anything in return. Here the forgiver "responds to hate with love" by "forgiving someone who does not deserve it."

Therefore, even though it increases her worth, the love is given as a gift. So, "gift" is the closest answer choice.
- **Choice A** is incorrect because "zealous" means enthusiastic or ardent support of a cause.
- **Choice B** is incorrect because "corpus" means a quantity or body (such as a body of literature).
- **Choice C** is incorrect because "exchange" is not as good of an answer choice as D ("gift"). In this context *provision* most nearly means to provide love without expecting or needing anything in return. Here the forgiver "responds to hate with love" by "forgiving someone who does not deserve it." Therefore, even though it increases her worth, the love is given as a gift. So, "give as a gift" is the closest answer choice.
- **Choice E** is incorrect because "mature" means grownup, established, or advanced.

RESEARCH **PREP.** GRE
www.research-prep.com

#12: The question was:

12. The tenacious owl kept his perch, despite the _____ fire.

A	flourishing
B	monotonous
C	noxious
D	commencing
E	sweeping
F	obvious

The correct answers are:

| A | flourishing; and |
| E | sweeping |

The sentence context shows:

The owl is described as tenacious for simply sitting on a branch; therefore, the fire must have been large. Less stubborn owls would have flown away already.

The answer choice vocabulary words and their synonyms are:

Answer Choice Vocabulary	Synonyms
Flourishing	Prospering, blooming
Monotonous	Boring, dull, remaining the same

The Verbal Reasoning and Analytical Writing Measures

Noxious	Deadly, harmful
Commencing	Begin, initiate
Sweeping	Wide-ranging, across-the-board, comprehensive
Obvious	Apparent, evident, understandable

#13: The question was:

13. Social distinctions or _____ are bad for societies that wish to foster democratic communities.

- [A] epidemics
- [B] hierarchies
- [C] demographics
- [D] classes
- [E] clamor
- [F] fundamentals

The correct answers are:

- [B] hierarchies; and
- [D] classes

The sentence context shows:

The goal of these societies is to have democratic communities, and social distinctions are bad for creating a democratic community. The context also shows that the correct answers should provide types of social distinctions.

The answer choice vocabulary words and their synonyms are:

Answer Choice Vocabulary	Synonyms
Epidemics	Widespread diseases
Hierarchies	Orders, rankings

Demographics	Statistics, population tally
Classes	Categories
Clamor	Loud cry, commotion
Fundamentals	Essentials, basics

#14: The question was:

14. The political candidate stated to the audience, that his speech would be (i)_____; it would only address a limited portion of the topic. He did this to (ii)_____ a previous statement in which he made a mistake, but still (iii)_____ his political opponent.

Blank (i)	Blank (ii)	Blank (iii)
(A) qualified	(D) ponder	(G) recast
(B) prominent	(E) recant	(H) refute
(C) motley	(F) muse over	(I) quandary

The correct answers are:

Blank (i):

(A) qualified

Blank (ii):

(E) recant

Blank (iii):

(H) refute

The answer choice vocabulary words and their synonyms are:

Answer Choice Vocabulary	Synonyms
Qualified	Restricted to a certain topic, limited
Prominent	Conspicuous, obvious, notable
Motley	Mixed, unmatched, many differences
Ponder	Consider, think, ruminate, muse over
Recant	Retract, disclaim, take back
Muse over	Consider, think, ruminate, ponder
Recast	Reconstruct, recreate to be better
Refute	Disprove, show the error in a claim
Quandary	Dilemma, question

#15: The question was:

15. The nun's _____ could not be mistaken; she was a true example of faithfulness and goodness.

- (A) fawning
- (B) piety
- (C) hyperbole
- (D) mnemonic
- (E) platitude

The correct answer is:

B piety

The answer choice vocabulary words and their synonyms are:

Answer Choice Vocabulary	Synonyms
Fawning	Flattering another, seeking to please another with kind behavior
Piety	Devoted to God, worshipful
Hyperbole	Exaggerating statement
Mnemonic	Involving memory, memory exercises
Platitude	Truism, common statement

#16: The question was:

16. Mountain climbing involves not only (i) _____ to work hard and a lack of (ii)_____ from an exercise plan, but also understanding how to deal with the elements and prevent harm to oneself from (iii)_____ while climbing mountains in difficult or changing conditions.

Blank (i)	Blank (ii)	Blank (iii)
A) taut	D) deviation	G) exposure
B) determination	E) rancor	H) regeneration
C) rendering	F) emergence	I) symbiosis

RESEARCH PREP. GRE
www.research-prep.com

The correct answers are:

Blank (i):

(B) determination

Blank (ii):

(D) deviation

Blank (iii):

(G) exposure

The answer choice vocabulary words and their synonyms are:

Answer Choice Vocabulary	Synonyms
Taut	Tight, stretched
Determination	Tenacity, single-mindedness, commitment
Rendering	Representation; deliver, provide
Deviation	Changing, diverging, rerouting
Rancor	Hatred, anger, bitterness
Emergence	Coming out, showing
Exposure	Harm from the elements, being outside, exposed to weather
Regeneration	Regrowth, rebirth
Symbiosis	Mutually interdependent relationship, often beneficial

Reading Comprehension Passage

The passage was:

RESEARCH PREP. GRE
www.research-prep.com

Rodeos are sometimes considered to be venues for the display of skills which, while exciting, are useless. However, learning the skills to control livestock is still crucial in many rural parts of the United States. Proponents of rodeos believe that by raising excitement for viewing expert displays of these skills in action, more young people will learn them. They believe this, in part, because more people will want to learn how to control livestock if it is seen as exciting to be good at it.

#17: The question was:

17. In this passage, the author's position is –

(A) that rodeos have proponents who believe they are necessary, but the author remains neutral.

(B) rodeos are necessary in many rural places within the United States.

(C) rodeos are exciting but useless.

(D) rodeos are exciting and either useless or crucial, but the author does not conclude either way.

(E) rodeos create reasons for young people to learn dangerous skills for entertainment.

The correct answer is:
(B) rodeos are necessary in many rural places within the United States.

This is why:
- **Choice B** is correct because the author articulates her argument in the second sentence: "...learning the skills to

control livestock is still crucial in many rural parts of the United States." This is the crucial sentence presenting the author's view.

The first sentence is the position to which the author is responding. ("Rodeos are sometimes considered to be venues for the display of skills which, while exciting, are useless.")

The third and fourth sentences are used by the author to support her argument. ("Proponents of rodeos believe that by raising excitement for viewing expert displays of these skills in action, more young people will learn them. They believe this, in part, because more people will want to learn how to control livestock if it is seen as exciting to be good at it.")

- **Choice A, C, D, and E** are incorrect because they all miss the author's clear thesis, which is presented in the second sentence: "...learning the skills to control livestock is still crucial in many rural parts of the United States." This is the crucial sentence presenting the author's view.

#18: The question was:

18. Based on the passage, each of the following is a reason proponents believe young people train to participate in rodeos EXCEPT –

(A) they are excited.
(B) they want to become experts.
(C) they have seen rodeos.
(D) they want to become fit.

(E) they want to learn skills.

The correct answer is:
(D) they want to become fit.

This is why:
- **Choice D** is correct because "they want to become fit" Is not stated in the passage as being part of the proponents' view.
- **Choice A** is incorrect because it is stated in the passage as "**raising excitement** for viewing expert displays of these skills in action, more young people will learn them" and "more people will want to learn how to control livestock if it is **seen as exciting** to be good at it."
- **Choice B** is incorrect because it is stated in the passage as "raising excitement for viewing **expert displays** of these skills in action, more young people **will learn them**."
- **Choice C** is incorrect because it is stated in the passage as by "raising excitement for **viewing** expert **displays** of these skills in action, more young people will learn them."
- **Choice E** is incorrect because it is stated in the passage as "more people **will want to learn how to control livestock** if it is seen as exciting to be good at it."

#19: The question was:

19. Which of these best sets forth the reason for the first two sentences of the passage?

(A) To explain a problem which needs a solution.

B) To explain that what is useless to one person may be crucial to another.

C) To showcase the difference between an urban view and a rural view on the same topic.

D) To succinctly present two sides of an ongoing argument.

E) To argue against rodeos and then change tactics and argue for them.

The correct answer is:
D) To succinctly present two sides of an ongoing argument.

This is why:
- **Choice D** is correct because the first sentence succinctly sets forth a position against rodeos and the author responds to it with a succinct articulation of a divergent position in the second sentence. From the wording of these sentences, it is also clear that these two sides are part of an ongoing argument. This answer choice (D) presents a better articulation of the first two sentences than any other answer choice.

#20: The question was:

20. Which of these actions, if performed, would help solve this debate?

A) The provision of information about the usefulness of rodeos by proponents to those who disagree.

(B) Continuing to have rodeos.

(C) Continuing to train for rodeos.

(D) Encouraging excitement for watching rodeos.

(E) Explaining the great danger of participating in a rodeo.

The correct answer is:
(A) The provision of information about the usefulness of rodeos by proponents to those who disagree.

This is why:
- **Choice A** is correct because it squarely addresses the other side of the argument with information showing the usefulness of rodeos. If they are then satisfied that rodeos are useful, their only argument (as presented in the passage) is addressed, and the debate is solved.
- **Choices B, C, and D** are incorrect because they do not address the perception of uselessness directly.
- **Choice E** is incorrect because it does not address the argument presented in the passage. It adds a new additional argument, which is not a part of the passage.

RESEARCH **PREP.** GRE

www.research-prep.com

Timed Practice Question Set #2

Time – 30 Minutes

GRE Instructions: Select the two answer choices that, when used to complete the sentence, fit the meaning of the sentence as a whole and produce completed sentences that are alike in meaning.

1. It is very _____ to achieve a high grade point average in graduate school.

- [A] garish
- [B] invigorating
- [C] mitigating
- [D] gratifying
- [E] harrowing
- [F] pleasing

2. He was _____ for days after she broke off their relationship; she had been worried that he was seeing someone else, but he was not.

- [A] pertinacious
- [B] morose

The Verbal Reasoning and Analytical Writing Measures

C	confused
D	sullen
E	mortified
F	skeptical

> GRE Instructions: For each blank select one entry from the corresponding column of choices. Fill all blanks in the way that best completes the text.

3. She spent so much time getting ready for the dance, that she was (i)_____ by his (ii)_____ appearance when he arrived to escort her.

Blank (i)	Blank (ii)
A) elated	D) traumatic
B) bolstered	E) disheveled
C) disheartened	F) garbled

4. The Judge told the bailiff to take the convict away despite the convict's heartfelt, _____, and penitent statement.

A) fallacious
B) contrite
C) blithe

D) convivial

E) anomalous

Reading Comprehension Passage

The professional resume is an opportunity to showcase your accomplishments and to connect your work history or academic background with the needs of your potential employer. Once you have identified the "type of position" that you are seeking, then, locate some readily available job listings (such as those online or in a trade publication). Look at the jobs to which you would want to apply and decide if your "type of position" has some variation.

Choose one correct answer choice.

5. In this context, the last sentence of this passage performs which of these functions?

A) To conclude a paragraph.

B) To summarize the main idea of a paragraph.

C) To transition the reader to the next idea, which will be set forth in greater detail in the following sentences.

D) To provide factual information upon which the reader can rely.

E) To explain the type of information, in part, which the reader might find in a job listing.

RESEARCH **PREP.** GRE

www.research-prep.com

> For this question, consider each answer choice separately and choose all correct answer choices.

6. Which of these statements is supported by the passage?

☐ A   Professional resumes explain to a potential employer the ways a candidate fits the position.

☐ B   Connecting with an employer is important, so excellent communication during interviews and involvement in networking is a good idea.

☐ C   A single type of position might at the same time have variation.

> Choose one correct answer choice for each question

7. Readers can infer from the passage that "potential employers" want, above all—

Ⓐ the smartest candidate.
Ⓑ the candidate with the best academic background.
Ⓒ the candidate with the most work history.
Ⓓ the most connected candidate.
Ⓔ the candidate who best fits the job description.

8. As used in the passage, "available" most nearly means –

Ⓐ up for grabs.
Ⓑ ready.

- C) open.
- D) can be found.
- E) looking for work.

9. The purpose of the author in writing this passage is to —

- A) instruct the reader.
- B) make an argument.
- C) discuss a topic.
- D) provide a forum for communication.
- E) engage the reader.

> GRE Instructions: Select the two answer choices that, when used to complete the sentence, fit the meaning of the sentence as a whole and produce completed sentences that are alike in meaning.

10. Her argument was _____; while it seemed plausible at first glance, it was inaccurate.

- A specious
- B sophisticated
- C misleading
- D wary
- E transient
- F irresolute

11. The salesman recommended the tile flooring as a good choice because it was _____ to water damage.

- [A] groundless
- [B] oblivious
- [C] dormant
- [D] impermeable
- [E] impervious
- [F] nondescript

12. The actor may _____ the director all day, but he will not get his way; he will only lose their good rapport.

- [A] waylay
- [B] rant at
- [C] rail against
- [D] stultify
- [E] jargon
- [F] exhort

GRE Instructions: For each blank select one entry from the corresponding column of choices. Fill all blanks in the way that best completes the text.

13. (i) _____ data is important to scientific inquiry, while intuition is seen as misleading. (ii)_____ scientific journals accept articles only when they are based on thorough research and have a demonstrated factual basis.

Blank (i)	Blank (ii)
A) Empirical	D) Blasé
B) Contentious	E) Erudite
C) Nebulous	F) Daunting

14. Please do not (i) _____ when you discuss these important details. Your (ii)_____ to lie must be tempered. I anger almost immediately when you (iii)_____.

Blank (i)	Blank (ii)	Blank (iii)
A) proliferate	D) fidelity	G) bastion
B) mollify	E) propensity	H) swelter
C) equivocate	F) misnomer	I) prevaricate

|289|

The Verbal Reasoning and Analytical Writing Measures

15. His play presented humans as despicable and vile. Therefore, critics called him a (i)_____. In actuality, he was just a bit contentious and (ii)_____. He certainly did not mean to (iii)_____ such troublesome reviews about his own character.

Blank (i)	Blank (ii)	Blank (iii)
(A) diatribe	(D) dupe	(G) foment
(B) drab	(E) droll	(H) divest
(C) misanthrope	(F) morose	(I) flout

Reading Comprehension Passage

In his work, The philosophy of horror, or, Paradoxes of the heart, Noël Carroll seeks to create a "theory of horror, which is conceived to be a genre that crosses numerous art forms and media." (Noël Carroll, The philosophy of horror, or, Paradoxes of the heart, Routledge 1990, p. 12, hereafter "Carroll"). He defines the term "art-horror" which includes literature, movies, and fine art. According to Carroll, a movie viewer can be art-horrified when, the viewer is screaming, tingling, or shuddering (or is otherwise physically agitated), and this was caused by thinking of a monster as possibly real. The monster is both threatening and disgusting (impure) to the viewer, and the viewer usually wants to avoid touching the monster. The monster can be any being that scientists do not think exists.

RESEARCH PREP. GRE
www.research-prep.com

Choose one correct answer choice for each question.

16. This passage is primarily concerned with –

(A) explaining how it feels to watch a horror movie.

(B) explaining Carroll's view.

(C) explaining how we feel when we think about a monster.

(D) explaining how emotional art can seem to some viewers or even readers.

(E) providing a balanced explanation of a unique form of art including, horror films, horror fiction, and horror art.

17. According to the passage, all of the following are true EXCEPT –

(A) Carroll believes a movie viewer can think of a monster, which is depicted in the movie, as possibly real.

(B) Carroll believes a movie viewer can feel threatened by a monster which is depicted in a movie.

(C) Carroll believes a movie viewer can feel like he wants to avoid touching the monster which is depicted in the movie.

(D) Carroll believes a movie viewer can become physically agitated when watching a horror movie.

(E) Carroll believes that monsters in movies include lizards, spiders, and other natural creatures.

18. What is the function of the first sentence of the passage?

(A) To introduce a controversial topic.

(B) To argue for horror as a type of art.

(C) To introduce a book, by an author, presenting a certain view.

(D) To take a stance that art is a broad category which has room for variety.

(E) To create an introduction for the discussion of emotional responses to unusual art.

19. The primary function of the last sentence is to –

(A) explain what a monster is.

(B) create a category into which a monster falls.

(C) create a category excluding monsters to explain they are any omitted being.

(D) explain that Carroll knows monsters are only found in the movies.

(E) further describe Carroll's view by explaining what a monster can be according to him.

20. It can be inferred from the passage that those who read Carroll's text probably –

(A) find the topic of "art-horror" interesting.

(B) agree with Carroll's view.

(C) are likely to disagree with Carroll's view.
(D) do not believe in monsters.
(E) like movies and possibly other unique forms of art.

ResearchPrep.GRE

Timed Practice Question Set #2
Answers and Explanations

#1: The question was:

1. It is very _____ to achieve a high grade point average in graduate school.

- [A] garish
- [B] invigorating
- [C] mitigating
- [D] gratifying
- [E] harrowing
- [F] pleasing

The correct answers are:

- [D] gratifying; and
- [F] pleasing

RESEARCH **PREP.** GRE
www.research-prep.com

The sentence context shows:

That the answers will likely either reflect the feeling of achievement once a high G.P.A. is achieved, or the feeling of hard work and difficulty required to achieve it.

The answer choice vocabulary words and their synonyms are:

Answer Choice Vocabulary	Synonyms
Garish	Gaudy, too bright, too vivid, too colorful
Invigorating	Energizing, motivating, exciting
Mitigating	Moderating, reducing, appeasing
Gratifying	Pleasing, satisfying
Harrowing	Agonizing, traumatic, overly stressful, distressing
Pleasing	Gratifying, favorable

#2: The question was:

2. He was _____ for days after she broke off their relationship; she had been worried that he was seeing someone else, but he was not.

- [A] pertinacious
- [B] morose
- [C] confused
- [D] sullen
- [E] mortified

|295|

The Verbal Reasoning and Analytical Writing Measures

RESEARCH PREP. GRE

www.research-prep.com

| F | skeptical |

The correct answers are:

| B | morose; and |
| D | sullen |

The sentence context shows:

She broke up with him because she was concerned that he was seeing another woman. However, he was not. He was exceedingly upset that she ended the relationship based on false information.

The answer choice vocabulary words and their synonyms are:

Answer Choice Vocabulary	Synonyms
Pertinacious	Persistent, stubborn
Morose	Melancholy, sullen, grumpy
Confused	Mixed up, disoriented, puzzled
Sullen	Brooding, upset, melancholy
Mortified	Horrified, surprisingly humiliated
Skeptical	Doubtful, not believing, without confirmation

#3: The question was:

3. She spent so much time getting ready for the dance, that she was (i)_____ by his (ii)_____ appearance when he arrived to escort her.

	Blank (i)		Blank (ii)
A	elated	D	traumatic
B	bolstered	E	disheveled
C	disheartened	F	garbled

The correct answers are:

Blank (i):

C) disheartened

Blank (ii):

E) disheveled

The answer choice vocabulary words and their synonyms are:

Answer Choice Vocabulary	Synonyms
Elated	Exuberant, happy
Bolstered	Increased, supported
Disheartened	Aggrieved, saddened
Traumatic	Harmful, fearful
Disheveled	Unkempt, messy
Garbled	Jumbled, distorted

RESEARCH PREP. GRE
www.research-prep.com

#4: The question was:

4. The Judge told the bailiff to take the convict away despite the convict's heartfelt, _____, and penitent statement.

(A)	fallacious
(B)	contrite

RESEARCH **PREP.** GRE
www.research-prep.com

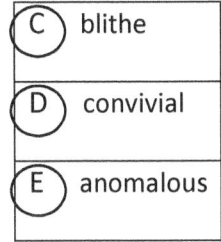

The correct answer is:

The answer choice vocabulary words and their synonyms are:

Answer Choice Vocabulary	Synonyms
Fallacious	False, misleading
Contrite	Penitent
Blithe	Carefree, unconcerned, unthinking
Convivial	Festive, jovial
Anomalous	Unusual, irregular, abnormal

Reading Comprehension Passage

The passage was:

The professional resume is an opportunity to showcase your accomplishments and to connect your work history or academic background with the needs of your potential employer. Once you have identified the "type of position" that you are seeking, then, locate some readily available job listings (such as those online or in a trade publication). Look at the jobs to which you would want to apply, and decide if your "type of position" has some variation.

#5: The question was:

5. In this context, the last sentence of this passage performs which of these functions?

(A) To conclude a paragraph.

(B) To summarize the main idea of a paragraph.

(C) To transition the reader to the next idea, which will be set forth in greater detail in the following sentences.

(D) To provide factual information upon which the reader can rely.

(E) To explain the type of information, in part, which the reader might find in a job listing.

The correct answer is:
(C) To transition the reader to the next idea, which will be set forth in greater detail in the following sentences.

This is why:
Choice C is the correct answer to this question. This sentence neither concludes the paragraph (Choice A) nor summarizes it (Choice B). It does provide a transition and prepares the reader for more detail, which will likely be set forth next (making Choice C correct). It does not provide either factual information (Choice D) or explanation (Choice E). It is more accurate to say that it provides instructions to be followed with a transition to additional information which will likely be set forth next.

RESEARCH PREP. GRE

www.research-prep.com

#6: The question was:

> For this question, consider each answer choice separately and choose all correct answer choices.

6. Which of these statements is supported by the passage?

| A | Professional resumes explain to a potential employer the ways a candidate fits the position.

| B | Connecting with an employer is important, so excellent communication during interviews and involvement in networking is a good idea.

| C | A single type of position might at the same time have variation.

The correct answers are:

| A | Professional resumes explain to a potential employer the ways a candidate fits the position.

| C | A single type of position might at the same time have variation.

This is why:
- **Choices A and C** are both correct because they are specifically supported by the passage. A is articulated in the text of the first sentence. C is set forth in the last sentence of the passage.
- **Choice B** is incorrect because B is neither explicitly nor implicitly communicated in the passage. While B may be a

true statement with which test takers agree, it is not "supported by the passage" as required by this test question.

#7: The question was:

7. Readers can infer from the passage that "potential employers" want, above all -

(A) the smartest candidate.

(B) the candidate with the best academic background.

(C) the candidate with the most work history.

(D) the most connected candidate.

(E) the candidate who best fits the job description.

The correct answer is:
(E) the candidate who best fits the job description.

This is why:
- **Choice E** is correct because the passage focuses more on connecting the candidate "...with the needs of [his] potential employer" (Choice E) than any other answer choice. While all of the answer choices can be helpful when job searching, this particular passage most fully seeks to connect the candidate's strengths with the employer's job description.
- **Choice A** is incorrect because it is not mentioned in the passage.
- **Choices B and C** are incorrect because, while they are very tempting, neither one is better than the other. However,

Choice E solves the problem by being a slightly better answer choice then these two.
- **Choice D** is incorrect because it is not mentioned in the passage.

RESEARCH **PREP.** GRE
www.research-prep.com

#8: The question was:

8. As used in the passage, "available" most nearly means –

- (A) up for grabs.
- (B) ready.
- (C) open.
- (D) can be found.
- (E) looking for work.

The correct answer is:
(D) can be found.

This is why:
- **Choice D** is correct because the job listings themselves can be found (or are available) in trade publications or online. None of the other answer choices match the meaning of "available" as used in this context.

#9: The question was:

9. The purpose of the author in writing this passage is to –

- (A) instruct the reader.
- (B) make an argument.
- (C) discuss a topic.
- (D) provide a forum for communication.

RESEARCH PREP. GRE
www.research-prep.com

(E) engage the reader.

The correct answer is:
(A) instruct the reader.

This is why:
- **Choice A** is correct because this passage provides specific instructions to the reader. It uses key phrases such as, "once you have…," "then," and "look at…" In the context of these phrases, the passage instructs the reader to follow certain sequential steps.
- **The other choices** are incorrect because they do not interpret the passage's text as accurately as Choice A does.

#10: The question was:

10. Her argument was _____; while it seemed plausible at first glance, it was inaccurate.

A	specious
B	sophisticated
C	misleading
D	wary
E	transient
F	irresolute

The Verbal Reasoning and Analytical Writing Measures

RESEARCH **PREP.** GRE

www.research-prep.com

The correct answers are:

|A| specious; and

|C| misleading

The sentence context shows:

Her argument was not accurate, but seemed so at first glance. This could mean that it was misleading or based on specious or erroneous reasoning.

The answer choice vocabulary words and their synonyms are:

Answer Choice Vocabulary	Synonyms
Specious	Incorrect despite seeming correct, misleading
Sophisticated	Urbane, knowing the ways of the world
Misleading	Seeming correct while inaccurate, purposeful or accidental misguidance
Wary	Cautious, regarding with suspicion, nervous about
Transient	Temporary, present only briefly, momentary
Irresolute	Uncertain, without resolve, wavering

#11: The question was:

11. The salesman recommended the tile flooring as a good choice because it was _____ to water damage.

A	groundless
B	oblivious
C	dormant
D	impermeable
E	impervious
F	nondescript

The correct answers are:

| D | impermeable; and |
| E | impervious |

The sentence context shows:

The tile was recommended because it would not become damaged by water easily.

The answer choice vocabulary words and their synonyms are:

Answer Choice Vocabulary	Synonyms
Groundless	Baseless, without reasons or evidence
Oblivious	Without noticing, unmindful of something due to absorption in another
Dormant	Latent, sleeping
Impermeable	Impenetrable, without passing through
Impervious	Invulnerable, impassable

| Nondescript | Without distinction, blends in, ordinary |

#12: The question was:

12. The actor may _____ the director all day, but he will not get his way; he will only lose their good rapport.

A. waylay

B	rant at
C	rail against
D	stultify
E	jargon
F	exhort

The correct answers are:

| B | rant at; and |
| C | rail against |

The sentence context shows:

The actor is doing something to the director which will not convince the director to give in, but will harm the actor's relationship with the director.

The answer choice vocabulary words and their synonyms are:

Answer Choice Vocabulary	Synonyms
Waylay	Hold over, hold up
Rant at	Yell at, argue with
Rail against	Criticize harshly
Stultify	Hinder, frustrate, show another's stupidity
Jargon	Technical terms, specialized terms, gibberish
Exhort	Urge, try to convince

RESEARCH **PREP.** GRE

www.research-prep.com

#13: The question was:

13. (i) _____ data is important to scientific inquiry, while intuition is seen as misleading. (ii)_____ scientific journals accept articles only when they are based on thorough research and have a demonstrated factual basis.

Blank (i)	Blank (ii)
A) Empirical	D) Blasé
B) Contentious	E) Erudite
C) Nebulous	F) Daunting

The correct answers are:

Blank (i):

A) Empirical

Blank (ii):

E) Erudite

The answer choice vocabulary words and their synonyms are:

Answer Choice Vocabulary	Synonyms
Empirical	Based in experience, from experience
Contentious	Quarrelsome, disagreeable, argumentative
Nebulous	Uncertain, vague, unwieldy

Blasé	Aloof, bored, disengaged emotionally
Erudite	Scholarly, learned
Daunting	Intimidating, nerve-wracking, looming

#14: The question was:

14. Please do not (i) _____ when you discuss these important details. Your (ii)_____ to lie must be tempered. I anger almost immediately when you (iii)_____.

	Blank (i)		Blank (ii)		Blank (iii)
A	proliferate	D	fidelity	G	bastion
B	mollify	E	propensity	H	swelter
C	equivocate	F	misnomer	I	prevaricate

The correct answers are:

Blank (i):

C) equivocate

Blank (ii):

E) propensity

Blank (iii):

I) prevaricate

RESEARCH **PREP.** GRE
www.research-prep.com

The answer choice vocabulary words and their synonyms are:

Answer Choice Vocabulary	Synonyms
Proliferate	Spread, multiply
Mollify	Soothe, placate
Equivocate	Waver
Fidelity	Loyalty, allegiance
Propensity	Inclination, innate
Misnomer	Inaccurate designation, incorrect name
Bastion	Protective fortification, stronghold
Swelter	To sweat from heat, oppressive heat
Prevaricate	Lie

#15: The question was:

15. His play presented humans as despicable and vile. Therefore, critics called him a (i)_____. In actuality, he was just a bit contentious and (ii)_____. He certainly did not mean to (iii)_____ such troublesome reviews about his own character.

Blank (i)	Blank (ii)	Blank (iii)
A) diatribe	D) dupe	G) foment
B) drab	E) droll	H) divest
C) misanthrope	F) morose	I) flout

The Verbal Reasoning and Analytical Writing Measures

The correct answers are:

Blank (i):

(C) misanthrope

Blank (ii):

(F) morose

Blank (iii):

(G) foment

The answer choice vocabulary words and their synonyms are:

Answer Choice Vocabulary	Synonyms
Diatribe	Argumentative statement, invective, scolding
Drab	Dull, lacks color, plain
Misanthrope	Person who hates others
Dupe	Gullible, easily fooled
Droll	Amusing
Morose	Sullen, melancholy, grumpy
Foment	Instigate
Divest	Remove, deprive, strip
Flout	Show contempt for, mock

Reading Comprehension Passage

The passage was:

RESEARCH PREP. GRE
www.research-prep.com

In his work, <u>The philosophy of horror, or, Paradoxes of the heart</u>, Noël Carroll seeks to create a "theory of horror, which is conceived to be a genre that crosses numerous art forms and media." (Noël Carroll, <u>The philosophy of horror, or, Paradoxes of the heart</u>, Routledge 1990, p. 12, hereafter "Carroll"). He defines the term "art-horror" which includes literature, movies, and fine art. According to Carroll, a movie-viewer can be art-horrified when, the viewer is screaming, tingling, or shuddering (or is otherwise physically agitated), and this was caused by thinking of a monster as possibly real. The monster is both threatening and disgusting (impure) to the viewer, and the viewer usually wants to avoid touching the monster. The monster can be any being that scientists do not think exists.

#16: The question was:

16. This passage is primarily concerned with –

(A) explaining how it feels to watch a horror movie.

(B) explaining Carroll's view.

(C) explaining how we feel when we think about a monster.

(D) explaining how emotional art can seem to some viewers or even readers.

(E) providing a balanced explanation of a unique form of art including, horror films, horror fiction, and horror art.

The correct answer is:
(B) explaining Carroll's view.

This is why:

- **Choice B** is correct, which is shown by these key phrases in the passage: "In his work...", "Carroll seeks to create a 'theory'...", "he defines the term...", and "[a]ccording to Carroll..." These phrases show us that the passage primarily aims to explain Carroll's view to the reader.
- **Choices A, C, D and E** are incorrect because they could be parts of Carroll's view, but each misses the main point of the passage, in favor of a feature that does not encompass the passage's overall purpose. The main point of the passage is to explain Carroll's view to the reader.

#17: The question was:

17. According to the passage, all of the following are true EXCEPT –

(A) Carroll believes a movie-viewer can think of a monster, which is depicted in the movie, as possibly real.

(B) Carroll believes a movie-viewer can feel threatened by a monster which is depicted in a movie.

(C) Carroll believes a movie-viewer can feel like he wants to avoid touching the monster which is depicted in the movie.

(D) Carroll believes a movie-viewer can become physically agitated when watching a horror movie.

(E) Carroll believes that monsters in movies include lizards, spiders, and other natural creatures.

The correct answer is:
(E) Carroll believes that monsters in movies include lizards, spiders, and other natural creatures.

This is why:
- **Choice E** is correct because the passage states that according to Carroll "[t]he monster can be any being that scientists do not think exists." Showing that Choice E is not a correct articulation of Carroll's view.
- **Choice A** is incorrect because it is stated in the passage as "and this was caused by thinking of a monster as possibly real."
- **Choice B** is incorrect because it is stated in the passage as "[t]he monster is both threatening and disgusting (impure) to the viewer…"
- **Choice C** is incorrect because it is stated in the passage as "the viewer usually wants to avoid touching the monster."
- **Choice D** is incorrect because it is stated in the passage as "the viewer is screaming, tingling, or shuddering (or is otherwise physically agitated)…"

#18: The question was:

18. What is the function of the first sentence of the passage?

(A) To introduce a controversial topic.

(B) To argue for horror as a type of art.

(C) To introduce a book, by an author, presenting a certain view.

(D) To take a stance that art is a broad category which has room for variety.

(E) To create an introduction for the discussion of emotional responses to unusual art.

The correct answer is:
(C) To introduce a book, by an author, presenting a certain view.

This is why:
- **Choice C** is correct because the first sentence specifically introduced a book by the author Noël Carroll, presenting a certain view (Carroll's "theory of horror"). Therefore, choice C is the correct answer. None of the other answer choices are as clear an explanation of the function of the first sentence.

#19: The question was:

19. The primary function of the last sentence is to —

(A) explain what a monster is.

(B) create a category into which a monster falls.

(C) create a category excluding monsters to explain they are any omitted being.

(D) explain that Carroll knows monsters are only found in the movies.

(E) further describe Carroll's view by explaining what a monster can be according to him.

The correct answer is:
(E) further describe Carroll's view by explaining what a monster can be according to him.

RESEARCH **PREP.** GRE
www.research-prep.com

This is why:
- **Choice E** is correct because the last sentence adds description to Carroll's view by telling the reader what a monster is according to Carroll. This is the best articulation of the function of the last sentence among the answer choices.

#20: The question was:

20. It can be inferred from the passage that those who read Carroll's text probably –

(A) find the topic of "art-horror" interesting.

(B) agree with Carroll's view.

(C) are likely to disagree with Carroll's view.

(D) do not believe in monsters.

(E) like movies and possibly other unique forms of art.

The correct answer is:
(A) find the topic of "art-horror" interesting.

This is why:
- **Choice A** is correct because by reading an entire book on the topic, readers likely show interest in the topic. It is at least more likely than the other answer choices, which makes it the best answer choice.
- **Choices B, C, and D** are incorrect because they are not as good as Choice A. It is more difficult to determine that they

agree with the view presented in the book (B), or disagree with the view presented in the book (C). Finally, we cannot tell whether they believe in monsters (D), and choice (D) also seems a little bit facetious (flippant or silly).
- **Choice E** is incorrect because, although it seems like a good choice, many people like movies and unique art, but dislike horror movies and horror art. So, choice A is preferable because it is more likely to be an accurate inference.

Chapter #5

The Analytical Writing Measure

(The Essay)

RESEARCH **PREP.** GRE
www.research-prep.com

THE ANALYTICAL WRITING MEASURE (THE ESSAY)

The analytical writing measure is the essay section on the GRE. The essays are always the first two sections of the test. You are required to write a total of two essays, one immediately after the other. You will have 30 minutes to write each essay, and each essay will have a different topic and a different set of instructions that you must follow. One essay will require you to "analyze an issue." The other essay will require you to "analyze an argument."

Analyze an Issue

This essay requires you to take a position on a topic. You will:

- Take a position on the issue;
- Articulate your position well;
- Discuss the intricacies of the issue, including addressing other perspectives with which you disagree;
- Argue for your view by providing reasons that your position is the best position; and
- Provide examples showing that you are right.

Analyze an Argument

This essay does not ask you to make an argument. It requires you to analyze the strengths and weaknesses of someone else's argument. One way to think about it is that you are critiquing the work of another. They have written an argument, and you are explaining its strengths and weaknesses, or filling in its logical gaps. You will:

- Analyze an argument already made in a passage;
- Critique the argument according to the instructions, for example, by:
    - Articulating its strengths and weaknesses;
    - Filling in the logical gaps in the argument;
    - Explaining the argument as you see it (how could it be made better, what are the problems you see); and/or
    - Providing examples showing how the argument is flawed or how your suggestions will improve it.

Follow the GRE Instructions

For both essays, the specific GRE instructions immediately following the question will vary. Make sure that you follow the instructions on your test and write on the topic presented to you. An essay that neither follows the instructions, nor addresses the topic presented, is given a score of 0.

Always Attribute

All work must be your own. Any plagiarism can result in the cancellation of your entire GRE score. If you paraphrase or quote, even from the GRE prompt itself, be smart and provide an attribution (a basic citation) to the source. Use quotation marks for three or more sequential words if they are not your own. Do not create written answer portions ahead of time with a study group. You do not want your answers to match that of another test-taker. GRE computer review programs may flag the same answers as plagiarized.

Score Highly

The essays are each graded on a scale, with 0 as the lowest possible score and 6 as the highest. Then, the two scores are averaged together, and you are given a single score reflecting both essays. For example, if one score is a 4 and one is a 5, your essay score is a 4.5.

These are the possible scores and what to do to achieve them:

An essay scoring a 6 or a 5.5 will contain:
- Complex ideas
- Logical analysis
- Persuasive writing
- Examples which are clearly supportive of the points made
- Excellent organization
- Effective vocabulary and sentence variation
- Excellent grammar (some small errors are acceptable)
- Quotation marks and basic citations as needed
- Content that addresses the topic and follows all of the instructions

An essay scoring a 5 or a 4.5 will contain:
- Complex ideas
- Logical analysis
- Good examples
- Effective organization
- Precise vocabulary and clear sentence structure
- Good grammar (some minor errors are acceptable)
- Quotation marks and basic citations as needed
- Content that addresses the topic and follows all of the instructions

An essay scoring a 4 or a 3.5 will contain:
- Competent ideas
- Competent analysis
- Relevant examples
- Adequate clarity and organization
- Satisfactory grammar (some larger errors are present)
- Quotation marks and basic citations as needed
- Content that addresses the topic and follows the instructions

An essay scoring a 3, 2.5, or 2 will contain:
- Some competence
- Limited development
- Limited organization
- Weak grammar
- Writing that has minor flaws and for lower scores lacks clarity
- Quotation marks and basic citations as needed
- Content that addresses the topic and follows the instructions

An essay scoring a 1.5, 1, or 0.5 will contain:
- Flawed writing
- Inadequate analysis
- Insufficient organization
- Grammatical problems
- Quotation marks and basic citations as needed
- Content that addresses the topic and follows the instructions

An essay scoring a 0 will contain:
- Content that does not address the topic
- Content that does not follow the instructions

- Plagiarism (it lacks necessary quotation marks or citations)

Keep in mind those things that you need to do to score highly. Now let's practice writing essays for the GRE.

Analyze an Issue Practice Questions

First, practice the "Analyze an Issue" essay. Remember, that you must:
- Take a position on the issue;
- Articulate your position well;
- Discuss the intricacies of the issue, including addressing other perspectives with which you disagree;
- Argue for your view by providing reasons that your position is the best position; and
- Provide examples showing that you are right.

Also seek to score as highly as possible by writing an essay containing:
- Complex ideas
- Logical analysis
- Persuasive writing
- Examples which are clearly supportive of the points made
- Excellent organization
- Effective vocabulary and sentence variation
- Excellent grammar (some small errors are acceptable)
- Content that addresses the topic and follows all of the instructions

RESEARCH **PREP.** GRE

www.research-prep.com

#1

Analyze an Issue
Practice Question

Time – 30 Minutes

ETS Directions: "You have 30 minutes to plan and compose a response to the issue below. A response to any other issue will receive a score of zero. Make sure that you respond according to the specific instructions and support your position on the issue with reasons and examples drawn from such areas as your reading, experience, observations, and/or academic studies."

> "We should not be so concerned with preserving traditions in our society. Innovative thinking is what improves our lives, not holding on to traditions."
>
> Respond in writing and state whether you agree or disagree with this statement. Support your position with reasons and examples. Also explain contrary viewpoints.

Analyze an Issue
Test-Taking Note

You may notice that this question is somewhat incongruous. "'Traditions" do not exactly juxtapose with "innovative thinking." When incongruity like this occurs on the GRE, consider how to create a juxtaposition that is on par.

For example, here you could try to develop "traditions" into "traditional thinking" for a better comparison to "innovative thinking." Some test-takers just make the leap to "traditional thinking." Others show the connection in the terms (clearly connecting "traditions" to "traditional thinking'"). Showing the connection that you are making is better if you can do it.

For example, you could do this by stating that some "traditions," such as wearing traditional clothing (traditional dress) increase sexual stereotypes. These stereotypes are connected to traditional ways of thinking about men and women. Then, you can take a position on "traditional thinking" as opposed to "innovative thinking," and you have created an example to use to prove your point.

Or, you could try to make leap from "traditions" to "traditional thinking" by stating that observing traditions (such as traditional meals or holidays) serve as reminders of past successes or mistakes. You could argue that these reinforce our thoughts about our culture, which constitute ways of "traditional thinking." Then, you can take a position on "traditional thinking" versus "innovative thinking."

Overall, beware of an inarticulate question, and consider ways to handle them by practicing. Expect that you may have to make a leap in thought to answer the question even when you are following the directions exactly.

Now practice writing your essay response for #1:

Analyze an Issue
Practice Question

Time – 30 Minutes

ETS Directions: "You have 30 minutes to plan and compose a response to the issue below. A response to any other issue will receive a score of zero. Make sure that you respond according to the specific instructions and support your position on the issue with reasons and examples drawn from such areas as your reading, experience, observations, and/or academic studies."

> Claim: "Experience, not beauty, is important in art; truly good art can show us something as though we were experiencing it."
>
> Supporting reason: "Art allows a person to glimpse a scene as seen from another's perspective."
>
> Please write your response stating whether you agree or disagree with the claim and its supporting reason. Provide a thorough explanation.

Analyze an Issue
Test-Taking Note

The beauty of a question which allows for interpretation is that you can choose how to answer it in a way that showcases your writing abilities. Here, you can choose to focus on the experiential qualities of art (the claim). Or focus more fully on how an artist conveys an idea to a viewer through the artwork (the supporting reason).

"Art" is also a broad term. You can write about fine art or attempt to bring in an example with which you are more familiar, such as a scene from a movie. Discussing a movie as an example of art can work to argue that experience is a quality of art and enable you to clearly communicate how one shares his perspective with others (such as describing ways a director shows his perspective to viewers).

A good technique can be to create an example with which you are familiar (such as movies) and use it to drive your overall answer.

Now practice writing your essay response for #2:

_____
_____
_____
_____
_____
_____

RESEARCH **PREP.** GRE
www.research-prep.com

#3

Analyze an Issue
Practice Question

Time – 30 Minutes

ETS Directions: "You have 30 minutes to plan and compose a response to the issue below. A response to any other issue will receive a score of zero. Make sure that you respond according to the specific instructions and support your position on the issue with reasons and examples drawn from such areas as your reading, experience, observations, and/or academic studies."

> "Every person should act responsibly; this means obeying authority and not resisting authority."
>
> Respond in writing and state whether you agree or disagree with this statement. Support your position with reasons and examples. Also explain contrary viewpoints.

RESEARCH **PREP.** GRE

www.research-prep.com

#4

Analyze an Issue
Practice Question

Time – 30 Minutes

ETS Directions: "You have 30 minutes to plan and compose a response to the issue below. A response to any other issue will receive a score of zero. Make sure that you respond according to the specific instructions and support your position on the issue with reasons and examples drawn from such areas as your reading, experience, observations, and/or academic studies."

> Claim: "Arguing with another person is generally a waste of time."
>
> Supporting reason: "Arguing destroys relationships and convincing another of a point involves persuasion, which is distinguishable from argument."
>
> Please write your response stating whether you agree or disagree with the claim and its supporting reason. Provide a thorough explanation.

#5

Analyze an Issue
Practice Question

Time – 30 Minutes

ETS Directions: "You have 30 minutes to plan and compose a response to the issue below. A response to any other issue will receive a score of zero. Make sure that you respond according to the specific instructions and support your position on the issue with reasons and examples drawn from such areas as your reading, experience, observations, and/or academic studies."

> Claim: "Laws are only just when they are applied consistently."
>
> Supporting reason: "Unjust application of a law, such as punishment of only certain groups and not others, undermines the fairness of the law itself."
>
> Please write your response stating whether you agree or disagree with the claim and its supporting reason. Provide a thorough explanation.

#6

Analyze an Issue
Practice Question

Time – 30 Minutes

ETS Directions: "You have 30 minutes to plan and compose a response to the issue below. A response to any other issue will receive a score of zero. Make sure that you respond according to the specific instructions and support your position on the issue with reasons and examples drawn from such areas as your reading, experience, observations, and/or academic studies."

> "A person should be kind to another when they first meet. We will never know what help we can be to another or what they can do for us if we are unkind at the outset of a relationship."
>
> Respond in writing and state whether you agree or disagree with this statement. Support your position with reasons and examples. Also explain contrary viewpoints.

#7

Analyze an Issue
Practice Question

Time – 30 Minutes

ETS Directions: "You have 30 minutes to plan and compose a response to the issue below. A response to any other issue will receive a score of zero. Make sure that you respond according to the specific instructions and support your position on the issue with reasons and examples drawn from such areas as your reading, experience, observations, and/or academic studies."

> Claim: "Deceiving another is not always wrong."
>
> Supporting reason: "For example, deceiving another is not wrong when we use a lie to manipulate another into doing something important."
>
> Please write your response stating whether you agree or disagree with the claim and its supporting reason. Provide a thorough explanation.

#8

Analyze an Issue
Practice Question

Time – 30 Minutes

ETS Directions: "You have 30 minutes to plan and compose a response to the issue below. A response to any other issue will receive a score of zero. Make sure that you respond according to the specific instructions and support your position on the issue with reasons and examples drawn from such areas as your reading, experience, observations, and/or academic studies."

> Claim: "In college, students should not strive toward a specific career path; instead, they should broaden their overall scope of knowledge."
>
> Supporting reason: "A liberal education through which a student increases his ability to think, read, and write will serve the student's later needs in life."
>
> Please write your response stating whether you agree or disagree with the claim and its supporting reason. Provide a thorough explanation.

The Verbal Reasoning and Analytical Writing Measures

#9

Analyze an Issue
Practice Question

Time – 30 Minutes

ETS Directions: "You have 30 minutes to plan and compose a response to the issue below. A response to any other issue will receive a score of zero. Make sure that you respond according to the specific instructions and support your position on the issue with reasons and examples drawn from such areas as your reading, experience, observations, and/or academic studies."

> "Relying on facts often proves ineffective. Scientific advancements generally prove that what we once believed, we should no longer hold to be true. What we think now to be 'fact,' later we see to be 'fiction.'"
>
> Draft an essay taking a position on this statement. Consider whether it is true or false and support your argument.

The Verbal Reasoning and Analytical Writing Measures

#10

Analyze an Issue
Practice Question

Time – 30 Minutes

ETS Directions: "You have 30 minutes to plan and compose a response to the issue below. A response to any other issue will receive a score of zero. Make sure that you respond according to the specific instructions and support your position on the issue with reasons and examples drawn from such areas as your reading, experience, observations, and/or academic studies."

> Claim: "Technological advancements have significantly improved education."
>
> Supporting reason: "Students and professionals can take courses online, enabling them to learn from professors and instructors who are significant in a field, but who do not teach locally."
>
> Please write your response stating whether you agree or disagree with the claim and its supporting reason. Provide a thorough explanation.

RESEARCH **PREP.** GRE
www.research-prep.com

#11

Analyze an Issue
Practice Question

Time – 30 Minutes

ETS Directions: "You have 30 minutes to plan and compose a response to the issue below. A response to any other issue will receive a score of zero. Make sure that you respond according to the specific instructions and support your position on the issue with reasons and examples drawn from such areas as your reading, experience, observations, and/or academic studies."

> Claim: "Honesty and effectiveness cannot always coexist in business."
>
> Supporting reason: "An effective businessman prioritizes increasing his company's market share, while an honest person maintains ethical standards that do not always create avenues for growth and can hinder them."
>
> Please write your response stating whether you agree or disagree with the claim and its supporting reason. Provide a thorough explanation.

#12

Analyze an Issue
Practice Question

Time – 30 Minutes

ETS Directions: "You have 30 minutes to plan and compose a response to the issue below. A response to any other issue will receive a score of zero. Make sure that you respond according to the specific instructions and support your position on the issue with reasons and examples drawn from such areas as your reading, experience, observations, and/or academic studies."

> "Progress requires us to recall the past; we must remember our mistakes to avoid repeating them. Studying history is important because it enables us to make progress without the hindrance of repeating our past mistakes."
>
> Draft an essay taking a position on this statement. Consider whether it is true or false and support your argument.

#13

Analyze an Issue
Practice Question

Time – 30 Minutes

ETS Directions: "You have 30 minutes to plan and compose a response to the issue below. A response to any other issue will receive a score of zero. Make sure that you respond according to the specific instructions and support your position on the issue with reasons and examples drawn from such areas as your reading, experience, observations, and/or academic studies."

> Claim: "Maintaining our freedom requires us to maintain a strong military."
>
> Supporting reason: "A strong military allows us to be self-directed without fearing (or encountering) encroachment from others."
>
> Please write your response stating whether you agree or disagree with the claim and its supporting reason. Provide a thorough explanation.

#14

Analyze an Issue
Practice Question

Time – 30 Minutes

ETS Directions: "You have 30 minutes to plan and compose a response to the issue below. A response to any other issue will receive a score of zero. Make sure that you respond according to the specific instructions and support your position on the issue with reasons and examples drawn from such areas as your reading, experience, observations, and/or academic studies."

> Claim: "Using technology to communicate increases our immediate accessibility; this helps us to connect with others more fully because we see their experience unfold."
>
> Supporting reason: "When we discuss an experience later, the depiction is more likely to be mediated rather than true to life."
>
> Please write your response stating whether you agree or disagree with the claim and its supporting reason. Provide a thorough explanation.

Analyze an Argument Practice Questions

Now, practice the "Analyze an Argument" essay. Remember that this essay does not ask you to make an argument. It requires you to analyze the strengths and weaknesses of someone else's argument. One way to think about it is that you are critiquing the work of another. They have written an argument, and you are explaining its strengths and weaknesses or filling in its logical gaps. You must:

- Analyze an argument already made in a passage;
- Critique the argument according to the instructions, for example, by:
  - Articulating its strengths and weaknesses;
  - Filling in the logical gaps in the argument;
  - Explaining the argument as you see it (how could it be made better, what are the problems you see); and/or
  - Providing examples showing how the argument is flawed or how your suggestions will improve it.

Also seek to score as highly as possible by writing an essay containing:

- Complex ideas
- Logical analysis
- Persuasive writing
- Examples which are clearly supportive of the points made
- Excellent organization
- Effective vocabulary and sentence variation
- Excellent grammar (some small errors are acceptable)

- Quotation marks and basic citations as needed
- Content that addresses the topic and follows all of the instructions

#15

Analyze an Argument
Practice Question

Time – 30 Minutes

ETS Directions: "You have 30 minutes to plan and compose a response in which you evaluate the argument passage that appears below. A response to any other argument will receive a score of zero. Make sure that you respond according to the specific instructions and support your evaluation with relevant reasons and/or examples. **Note that you are NOT being asked to present your own views on the subject**."

This was published by Weight Management Magazine:

Weight management is crucial to American health. Health experts say only 50% of citizens are at a healthy weight. But health experts unfortunately equate movie-going with weight gain. People who go to the movies often are not in a different weight category than the general public. Therefore, going to the movies does not cause weight gain. Additionally, movies are expensive, and people who can afford them can also afford weight management programs. An increase in weight management program purchasing will help to improve weight management in America.

Draft a response. In your response, examine the assumptions underlying the argument and explain how these unstated assumptions provide a basis for the argument. Also explain the implications for the argument if the unstated assumptions, upon which it is based, are unwarranted.

Analyze an Argument
Test-Taking Note

Consider including analysis of these ideas when creating your essay:

- First, the problem is stated as "Health experts say only 50% of citizens are at a healthy weight."
- Second, the argument was published by Weight Management Magazine.
- Third, the goal is stated in the concluding line of the argument as "[a]n increase in weight management program purchasing will help to improve weight management in America."
- Fourth, this may be being argued for the purpose of increased profit by the company making the argument (Weight Management Magazine).
    - Consider if a profit motive is a negative here, or if it is okay for the magazine to have a self-serving motivation for the argument.
- Fifth, consider if there is a distracting focus in the argument involving the movies, which may act to hide the profit motive.
    - Consider analyzing the movie idea; it will require you to bring in a great deal of your own analysis, so think about whether this is a good idea for your essay. Will it be better to focus on it as a distraction or to focus on the merits of the movie argument itself?

Now practice writing your essay response for #15:

#16

Analyze an Argument
Practice Question

Time – 30 Minutes

ETS Directions: "You have 30 minutes to plan and compose a response in which you evaluate the argument passage that appears below. A response to any other argument will receive a score of zero. Make sure that you respond according to the specific instructions and support your evaluation with relevant reasons and/or examples. **Note that you are NOT being asked to present your own views on the subject.**"

This was printed in Soccer Weekly:

Doctors are studying physical fitness in America. They say only 25% of Americans are fit. 30 years ago, 50% of people were fit under the physicians' prior standard for gauging fitness. Physicians originally thought that the current lack of fitness was due to computer use and an associated high work ethic. But they have changed their theory upon learning that computer users have much higher fitness levels than non-computer users. Soccer Weekly has noticed a 25% decline in adult soccer team registration. Therefore, fitness levels are likely to increase when team sport registration and associated playing returns to prior levels.

Draft a response. In your response, examine the assumptions underlying the argument and explain how these unstated assumptions provide a basis for the argument. Also explain the implications for the argument if the unstated assumptions, upon which it is based, are unwarranted.

#17

Analyze an Argument
Practice Question

Time – 30 Minutes

ETS Directions: "You have 30 minutes to plan and compose a response in which you evaluate the argument passage that appears below. A response to any other argument will receive a score of zero. Make sure that you respond according to the specific instructions and support your evaluation with relevant reasons and/or examples. **Note that you are NOT being asked to present your own views on the subject.**"

> A lake community boat club provided this recommendation to their readers: "The lake community boat club recommends that swimmers stay toward the shallow sides of the lake, near the sandy public beaches. This is because only 25% of lake swimmers are able to swim in deep water for over 10 minutes. (This is based on a national survey of boaters.) When a swimmer is having difficulty in deep waters, boats sailing by may worsen the swimmer's plight if the boaters do not spot the swimmer. We think this may be because boats can create waves, which could engulf the swimmer (as occurred in one incident in a neighboring

|458|

state last year). Because most swimmers are not very strong, they should stick close to the shore or stay on a boat. This will increase safety in our lake community."

Draft a response. In your response examine the assumptions underlying the argument and explain how these unstated assumptions provide a basis for the argument. Also explain the implications for the argument if the unstated assumptions, upon which it is based, are unwarranted.

#18

Analyze an Argument
Practice Question

Time – 30 Minutes

ETS Directions: "You have 30 minutes to plan and compose a response in which you evaluate the argument passage that appears below. A response to any other argument will receive a score of zero. Make sure that you respond according to the specific instructions and support your evaluation with relevant reasons and/or examples. **Note that you are NOT being asked to present your own views on the subject**."

> The morning paper printed this advertisement for Creamery's contest: "It's National Ice Cream Day today! Come downtown to join in an event at the farmer's market. Our neighboring town's favorite local ice cream shop, Creamery, will host a contest to see who can eat the most ice cream in 10 minutes. The entry fee is only $10. There are four contest times available: 11:00 a.m., 12:00 p.m., 1:00 p.m., and 2:00 p.m. The winner of each context will receive a coupon for a free ice cream to be used anytime next year. Because it is National Ice Cream Day, do your duty as a

resident of our town and eat ice cream! You will have fun and be happy if you eat ice cream on National Ice Cream Day!"

Draft a response. In your response, examine the assumptions underlying the argument and explain how these unstated assumptions provide a basis for the argument. Also explain the implications for the argument if the unstated assumptions, upon which it is based, are unwarranted.

#19

Analyze an Argument
Practice Question

Time – 30 Minutes

ETS Directions: "You have 30 minutes to plan and compose a response in which you evaluate the argument passage that appears below. A response to any other argument will receive a score of zero. Make sure that you respond according to the specific instructions and support your evaluation with relevant reasons and/or examples. **Note that you are NOT being asked to present your own views on the subject**."

A school board member is trying to convince residents to participate in a contest. Her flyer tells the community: "Our town is having a contest! The money raised will benefit the school construction project in a neighboring town. The contest has no entry fee, and if you participate, you can win a prize! Our community will be stronger if our schools are better. Come to town and enter the contest!"

Draft a response. In your response, examine the argument, and explain how the argument can be strengthened by filling in the gaps in the reasoning of the argument.

#20

Analyze an Argument
Practice Question

Time – 30 Minutes

ETS Directions: "You have 30 minutes to plan and compose a response in which you evaluate the argument passage that appears below. A response to any other argument will receive a score of zero. Make sure that you respond according to the specific instructions and support your evaluation with relevant reasons and/or examples. **Note that you are NOT being asked to present your own views on the subject**."

> Collectors of posters advertising rock music concerts especially appreciate rock band posters showcasing original artwork created to advertise a new tour. Recently, a few new bands have used poster art to showcase concert tours. These bands are predicted to increase in popularity more quickly than other new bands who do not create posters with original art backdrops for their tour advertisements.
>
> Draft a response to this prediction identifying the questions that need answers to allow you to decide if the prediction is reasonable. Explain how answering the questions would help evaluate the prediction.

#21

Analyze an Argument
Practice Question

Time – 30 Minutes

ETS Directions: "You have 30 minutes to plan and compose a response in which you evaluate the argument passage that appears below. A response to any other argument will receive a score of zero. Make sure that you respond according to the specific instructions and support your evaluation with relevant reasons and/or examples. **Note that you are NOT being asked to present your own views on the subject**."

> Native American tools, such as original handmade arrowheads can be expensive collectors' items. Recently, arrowheads which are machine produced, modern imitations have been created to increase gift store replica sales. These have, in fact, become increasingly popular. These replicas are regularly purchased by visitors to national parks and by online customers. Because replica arrowhead sales have drastically increased, merchants predict that rare, authentically Native American arrowheads will increase in value as well.

Draft a response to this prediction identifying the questions that need answers to allow you to decide if the prediction is reasonable. Explain how answering the questions would help evaluate the prediction.

RESEARCH **PREP.** GRE
www.research-prep.com

#22

Analyze an Argument
Practice Question

Time – 30 Minutes

ETS Directions: "You have 30 minutes to plan and compose a response in which you evaluate the argument passage that appears below. A response to any other argument will receive a score of zero. Make sure that you respond according to the specific instructions and support your evaluation with relevant reasons and/or examples. **Note that you are NOT being asked to present your own views on the subject**."

> Large cruise ships resemble resorts to their vacationers. A typical cruise ship can weigh over 92,000 tons and accommodate 4,000 passengers (including vacationers and crew members) for weeks at a time. They even have on board casinos for vacationers' pleasure. Land resorts, such as those in Las Vegas, also seem to maximize excitement and size to attract vacationers. Based on these current examples, we can predict that vacationing in national park campgrounds is at an all-time low.

Draft a response to this prediction identifying the questions that need answers to allow you to decide if the prediction is reasonable. Explain how answering the questions would help evaluate the prediction.

Analyze an Argument
Practice Question

Time – 30 Minutes

ETS Directions: "You have 30 minutes to plan and compose a response in which you evaluate the argument passage that appears below. A response to any other argument will receive a score of zero. Make sure that you respond according to the specific instructions and support your evaluation with relevant reasons and/or examples. **Note that you are NOT being asked to present your own views on the subject**."

> Turn-of-the-century vases, once thought to be hand-created by artisans and expert craftsmen, have now been discovered to have been created in batches by laborers. They used molds for quick reproduction of skilled unique creations. Because of their popularity and the fact that early artistic reproductions are themselves rare, their value is predicted to decline only a small amount at first. But, overtime as they become known to be reproductions of skilled unique vases, their value is likely to decline more significantly.

Draft a response to this prediction identifying the questions that need answers to allow you to decide if the prediction is reasonable. Explain how answering the questions would help evaluate the prediction.

#24

Analyze an Argument
Practice Question

Time – 30 Minutes

ETS Directions: "You have 30 minutes to plan and compose a response in which you evaluate the argument passage that appears below. A response to any other argument will receive a score of zero. Make sure that you respond according to the specific instructions and support your evaluation with relevant reasons and/or examples. **Note that you are NOT being asked to present your own views on the subject.**"

> Movie tickets are believed to be expensive by many would be movie-goers. Recently, a local theater owner decided to drop ticket prices and concentrate on profiting from popcorn and candy sales. His experiment will only pay off if popcorn and candy sales rise. He predicts that this will occur because regular customers will have more money to spend on concessions, and low ticket prices will attract new customers to his theater over competitors. These new customers will also increase popcorn and candy sales. Competitors predict that lowering ticket prices will fail to increase profits. They believe that movie-goers will go

to see the show and save the extra money, rather than spending it on popcorn.

Draft a response to these predictions identifying the questions that need answers to allow you to decide if the predictions are reasonable. Explain how answering the questions would help evaluate the predictions.

#25

Analyze an Argument
Practice Question

Time – 30 Minutes

ETS Directions: "You have 30 minutes to plan and compose a response in which you evaluate the argument passage that appears below. A response to any other argument will receive a score of zero. Make sure that you respond according to the specific instructions and support your evaluation with relevant reasons and/or examples. **Note that you are NOT being asked to present your own views on the subject.**"

> The candidate for mayor stated: "Research regarding job searching indicates that although networking is perceived to be an important, even crucial part of a job search, the use of networking techniques by a job-searcher does not increase the likelihood of being hired. While not discussed in the research, this appears to be because job searchers often use networking techniques that are ineffective. Therefore, our community should create programs showing job seekers how to properly network. This suggestion is superior to my opponent's

suggestion that more jobs need to be created by boosting the economy for the unemployment rate to decline."

Write an essay discussing the evidence that you would use to choose the better suggestion.

RESEARCH **PREP.** GRE
www.research-prep.com

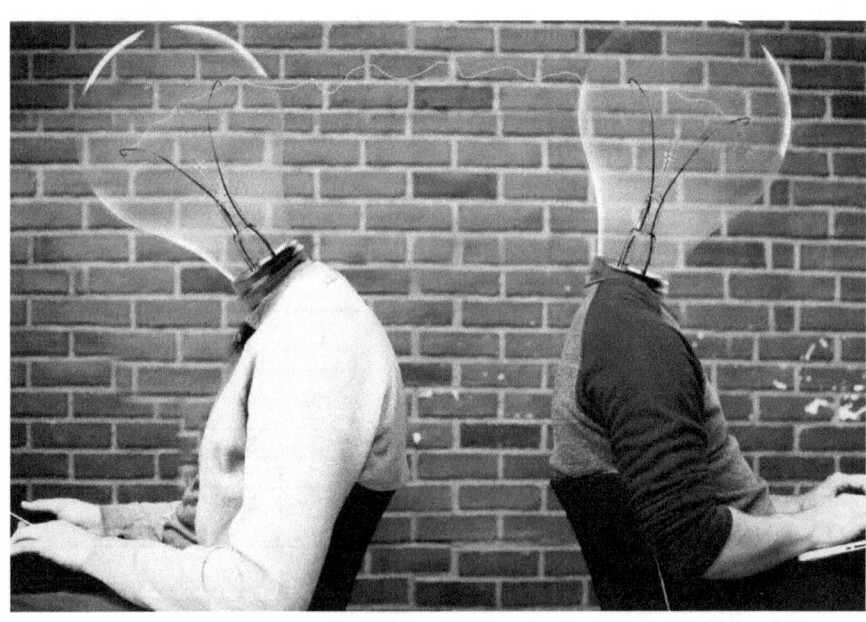

Chapter #6

Timed Essay Question Practice Set

Analyze an Issue

Time – 30 Minutes

ETS Directions: "You have 30 minutes to plan and compose a response to the issue below. A response to any other issue will receive a score of zero. Make sure that you respond according to the specific instructions, and support your position on the issue with reasons and examples drawn from such areas as your reading, experience, observations, and/or academic studies."

> Claim: "Original works of art are less valuable when we distribute prints and pictures of them."
>
> Supporting reason: "When there is only one of something, its rarity increases its value."
>
> Please write your response stating whether you agree or disagree with the claim and its supporting reason. Provide a thorough explanation.

_____
_____
_____
_____
_____
_____
_____
_____
_____

RESEARCH **PREP.** GRE
www.research-prep.com

Analyze an Issue
Review Your Answer

Correct your answer by considering if your essay fulfills your goals, which are to:
- Take a position on the issue;
- Articulate your position well;
- Discuss the intricacies of the issue, including addressing other perspectives with which you disagree;
- Argue for your view by providing reasons that your position is the best position; and
- Provide examples showing that you are right.

The highest scoring essays will contain all of these:
- Complex ideas
- Logical analysis
- Persuasive writing
- Examples that are clearly supportive of the points made
- Excellent organization
- Effective vocabulary and sentence variation
- Excellent grammar (some small errors are acceptable)
- Content that addresses the topic and follows all of the instructions

Analyze an Argument

Time – 30 Minutes

ETS Directions: "You have 30 minutes to plan and compose a response in which you evaluate the argument passage that appears below. A response to any other argument will receive a score of zero. Make sure that you respond according to the specific instructions and support your evaluation with relevant reasons and/or examples. **Note that you are NOT being asked to present your own views on the subject**."

> Large footprints were found in an area near the Florida coastline. Also present were blood splotches, and witnesses reported having heard loud screeching sounds early that morning. Upon further investigation, scientists found white and black feathers. Some of the scientists believe that two *Pelecanuserythrorhynchos* (American white pelicans) became embroiled in a fight. However, others believe that two birds of different species are more likely to have clashed, such as a *Cygnus buccinator* (Trumpeter swan) and a *Pelecanuserythrorhynchos* (American white pelican). Those scientists argue this, in part, because many more white feathers were found than black feathers. Other species were potentially present like the northern gannet (*Morusbassanus*) or Ross's goose (*Anserrossii*).
>
> Write an essay discussing the evidence that you would use to choose the better suggestion.

RESEARCH **PREP.** GRE

www.research-prep.com

Analyze an Argument Review Your Answer

Remember that this essay does not ask you to make an argument. It requires you to analyze the strengths and weaknesses of someone else's argument or fill in its logical gaps. Correct your answer by considering if your essay fulfills your goals, which are to:
- Analyze an argument already made in a passage;
- Critique the argument according to the instructions, for example, by:
    - Explaining the argument as you see it (including the problems you see with choosing a suggestion based on the incomplete evidence);
    - Filling in the logical gaps in the argument. Here, this requires you to explain the evidence which you could use to choose the better suggestion;
    - Providing examples showing how the argument is flawed and how your suggested additional evidence will improve your ability to identify and choose a suggestion;
    - Articulating how your revisions will help you to choose the better suggestion.

The highest scoring essays will contain all of these:
- Complex ideas
- Logical analysis
- Persuasive writing
- Examples which are clearly supportive of the points made
- Excellent organization
- Effective vocabulary and sentence variation

- Excellent grammar (some small errors are acceptable)
- Quotation marks and basic citations as needed
- Content that addresses the topic and follows all of the instructions

Chapter #7

HOW THE TEST WORKS

HOW THE TEST WORKS

The GRE stands for "Graduate Record Examination." It is a computer-based test with some paper-based formats available (in limited circumstances and locations). There are three topics covered by the GRE: (1) Analytical Writing Measure (essay writing); (2) Verbal Reasoning Measure (questions primarily involving reading comprehension, vocabulary, and some logical analysis); and (3) Quantitative Reasoning Measure (math).

The Analytical Writing Measure is always the first measure you encounter on the test. This means that you will draft both 30-minute essay tasks first. You will type each essay into a computer format that does not have a spelling or grammar-checking program. You will be able to delete text you type and cut and paste your own text to organize each essay. You will have 30 minutes for the "analyze an issue" essay task immediately followed by 30 minutes for the "analyze an argument" essay task.

After the essays, you will encounter question sets. There will be two sections of the Verbal Reasoning Measure. Each section allows you 30 minutes to answer approximately 20 questions. There are also two Quantitative Reasoning Measures; each section allows you 35 minutes to solve approximately 20 questions. There is also an experimental section, which is not graded. However, it looks like either an additional Verbal Reasoning Measure or an additional Quantitative Reasoning Measure. You will not be able to identify it as the experimental section, so you must treat it as a graded test section. Overall, there will be five sets of questions including the experimental section.

There is also the possibility of an optional research section, which you can choose to participate in or decline at the end of the test. It does not change your text score. After the test ends, you may send your scores to up to four schools from the GRE testing terminal where you have taken the test. You may not bring anything with you, just an idea of where you would like to send your scores.

Finally, choose to accept (or cancel) your score!

The GRE Proceeds Like This

30 minutes	First Essay Task One Question
30 minutes	Second Essay Task One Question
One minute break	
30 minutes if Verbal Reasoning 35 minutes if Quantitative	Question Set 20 Questions (verbal or math)
One minute break	
30 minutes if Verbal Reasoning 35 minutes if Quantitative	Question Set 20 Questions (verbal or math)
10 minute break	You can generally use this as a break to leave your computer, but make sure to follow the rules in your test center (for example, you may be required to raise your hand.
30 minutes if Verbal Reasoning 35 minutes if Quantitative	Question Set 20 Questions (verbal or math)
One minute break	
30 minutes if Verbal Reasoning 35 minutes if Quantitative	Question Set 20 Questions (verbal or math)
One minute break	
30 minutes if Verbal Reasoning 35 minutes if Quantitative	Question Set 20 Questions (verbal or math)

The Verbal Reasoning and Analytical Writing Measures

Input schools to which you would like ETS to send your score	You do not yet know your score when you input this information.
Choose to accept (or cancel) your GRE score	You do not see your score until you make this choice.
SEE YOUR GRE SCORE!	You will only see your numerical raw score if you choose to accept it. Essay scores arrive with scaled score results. You will not see a canceled score (and cannot learn it later).

Choosing to Accept Your Score

If you accept your score, you will see your raw numerical score on the computer screen a few moments after choosing to accept it. You will receive your essay score with your scaled score (which is close to the raw score) a couple of weeks later. You will not see any score if you cancel it (and you cannot obtain it later).

The computer will simply ask you if you would like to accept your score. Accepting your score means that it will be used for graduate admissions purposes. If you do not accept your score, you cannot use it and you must re-take the test if you plan to apply to graduate school. This is called cancelling your score.

You choose whether to accept or cancel your score before you know what the score is. Generally, choose to accept the score unless something went very wrong while taking your test. Many test-takers underestimate their score immediately following the test. You will only see the score if you accept it. You never see a cancelled score.

The analytical writing section is also scored separately. Each of the two essays are scored and then averaged together. Your essay score will be sent with your scaled score in about two weeks if you accept your GRE score on test day. You will not see your Analytical Writing Measure score on test day after accepting your score. You will only receive your scores for the Verbal Reasoning and Quantitative Reasoning Measures.

GRE Score Ranges

Verbal Reasoning Measure	130–170 (gauged in one point increments)
Quantitative Reasoning Measure	130–170 (gauged in one point increments)
Analytical Writing Measure	0–6 (gauged in half point increments)

A Multi-Stage Test Means Question Difficulty Adjusts

The GRE is a multi-stage test. This means that if you perform better on an earlier section, you are given harder questions in the next section of that type. For example, doing well in the first Verbal Reasoning Measure question bank will make the computer give you a harder second Verbal Reasoning Measure question bank. Your Verbal Reasoning score is based on both the number of questions you get right and how difficult your questions were.

So, be happy if the questions are tougher in the second Verbal Reasoning Measure question bank or tougher in the second Quantitative Reasoning Measure question bank. The tougher questions you receive in the second section, the higher your potential score can be!

Verbal Section One	**Verbal Section two is harder...** If your scores were excellent on verbal section one.
	Verbal Section two is moderate... If scores were moderate on verbal section one.
	Verbal Section two is easier... If your scores were lower on verbal section one.
Math Section One	**Math Section two is harder...** If your scores were excellent on math section one.
	Math Section two is moderate... If scores were moderate on math section one.
	Math Section two is easier... If your scores were lower on math section one.

Answer Every Question

Make sure to answer every question on the GRE. When you are uncertain, but need to move on due to time constraints then guess. You can also use the "mark button" to flag that question. This means that if you finish the section with time to spare, then you can review a list of questions you have "marked" in the review section. You can then return to that question and give it further consideration.

It is important to answer every question, so if you are uncertain then guess. You want to complete the entire section and answer every question.

Do not exit the section or quit the test before your time expires. Just keep trying for your best score. Or sit and rest while time expires for that section to receive a few extra minutes of break time.

Registration

Register for the GRE online at www.ets.org/gre. It is available in many countries on an ongoing basis. The test costs about $205 (US), and you must register in advance. Requests for accommodations can be made online.

Test Day

On test day, remember to bring all documentation required by ETS (the writers of the GRE) and your testing center. Check www.ets.org/gre for instructions regarding what to bring (usually photo ID and your ETS voucher, maybe in a clear plastic bag).

Arrive early for your testing time. Test centers are often hidden in office complexes or shopping areas (such as under or over a bank or store). They are sometimes hard to find and can, at times, be overwhelmed with people. If it is very busy at your test center, you may be required to wait to test.

The test site will provide scratch paper and pencils for you to use. There is a computer calculator for the math sections, but you may not bring your own.

www.ingramcontent.com/pod-product-compliance
Lightning Source LLC
Chambersburg PA
CBHW082032230426
43670CB00016B/2631